Div

MW00901732

Ten Steps to Preventing a
Divorce and Save Your Marriage

are for clarifying purposes only and are the owned by the owners themselves, not affiliated with this document.

Check Out My Other Books!

Thanks for downloading my book! I am a firm believer that in order to have a fulfilling family life-one must be properly prepared and understand the fundamentals of relationships, how to be a good parent, and live an exciting and adventurous sex life. As you can see, I have written a series of multiple books on marriage, sex, and parenting. If you are looking to learn more about how to improve your marriage, sex and dating life, family life, etc.-please check out my other books! Simply click on the links below or search the titles below to check them out.

Parenting:

Parenting 101: 20 strategies to follow to raise well-behaved children

Raising Your Kids: Time Management for Parents for Stress-Free Parenting

Sex (General):

Sex Positions: Your Guide to the 50 Best Sex Positions for a sexy marriage!

Tantra Sex: The Beginner's Guide to 25 Tantra Techniques

Tantric Massage: Your Guide to the Best 30 Tantric Massage Techniques

BDSM Positions: The Beginner's Guide to 30 BDSM Techniques

Sex: Spice Up Your Sex Life! How to be maintain an awesome sex life with your partner and live your wildest sexual fantasies!

Sex Games: 35 Naughty Sex Games to make your Sex Life Hot!

Sex For Women:

Sexting: Sexting Tips for Women: 100 tips to turn him on!

Sex Positions for Women: The Ultimate Guide to the 50 Best Techniques to Turn Your Man On!

Talk Dirty: How to talk to get your man aroused and in the mood for sex!

Sex: The Hottest Tips for Better Orgasms!

Sex for Men:

Sex Positions for Men: The Ultimate Guide to the 50 Best Techniques to Turn Her On!

Dirty Talk: Talking Dirty for Men: 200 Examples to Get Your Girl Aroused and in the Mood for Sex!

Sex: Make her beg for more and be the best she's ever been with in bed!

Marriage:

Dating:

Contents

Introduction

I want to thank you and congratulate you for downloading the book, *"Divorce: Ten Steps to Prevent a Divorce and Save Your Marriage"*.

This book contains proven steps and strategies on how to apply the fundamentals of building a strong marriage, avoid the common causes of divorce, and

Marriage is defined as a process where two individuals solidify their union, but in this society where divorce cases have continuously increased in number, the words "official" and "permanent" don't seem to mean as much as they used to. Are you really ready to accept that marriage is a dying institution? Through this book, you'll learn how to prevent your marriage from going down the divorce path.

Marriage is not for wimps. A marriage is truly over only when two people have ceased to love each other and not because they've encountered a crisis or two. Conflicts are normal in marriages. They can either ruin a marriage or make it stronger. However, it's not the nature of the problem that determines the kind of impact it'll have on your relationship. It's the way through which you handle the problem together, as a couple.

Through this book, you will learn practical strategies on how to avoid a divorce. A successful marriage is made up of a bunch of routines. It's what makes everything function and fit together. However, when routine finds its way into the bedroom, there can be no faster way to kill passion. Through these pages, you'll find tips on how to rekindle the fire in the hearth *and* between the sheets.

Thanks again for downloading this book, I hope you enjoy it!

Chapter 1 - What are the Fundamentals of a Strong Marriage?

Don't make promises you can't keep.

Marriages are based on promises right from the moment the couples say their vows. Therefore, you can't blame your spouse if he/she has developed certain expectations. When people are in love, they're ready to promise just about anything. However, failure to turn promises into reality can easily lead to frustration, mistrust and resentment. Keep it real. You don't have to promise him/her the moon and the stars. Instead, offer your spouse whatever you can give and whatever you're willing to give. Before making a promise to your partner, ask yourself: will I be able to keep my word when things go smoothly *and* when things go bad?

Happiness is something that you create.

Most couples make the mistake of thinking that happiness is a byproduct of marriage. In a way, it is, but here's the catch - you have to make it yourself. Happiness is something that you strive to achieve on a daily basis. It depends on your daily words, actions and choices. Successful married couples are able to learn to *intentionally* draw in happiness to their marriage by creating one beautiful memory after another. This entails effort, patience, understanding, openness and sharing. But more than that, they *do* things that can help bring happiness back into the marriage when the inevitable realities of life try to take that happiness away.

Love is not just a noun. It's also a verb.

At first, marriage creates this feel-good sensation. Newlywed couples live inside this bubble where everything seems possible as long as they're in love and together, but the thing is, love is not just a feeling. It's all about what you do when that bubble is punctured and you and your spouse are exposed to the realities of married life.

Get rid of "the grass is greener" mentality.

Quit entertaining thoughts like "Maybe I'll be happier with someone else." Or "Maybe I should've married my high school sweetheart instead…" etc. When your marriage is going through a rough patch, it's tempting to wonder about what-might-have-beens. As much as possible, you'd like to think that it's not your fault that your marriage is not up to fairy-tale standards. However, successful married couples have learned to understand that the grass is always greenest wherever you take care of it; thus, they invest time and energy into improving themselves and their marriage.

Doing the same old things lead to the same old results.

Smart couples understand the importance of exploring various approaches to address a problem. They don't make the mistake of applying the same old solution that has failed them in the past. They know that doing so will only lead to further disappointment and hopelessness. Sometimes, a small change in attitude or a mere modification of action can make a tremendous difference. Furthermore, fixing marriage issues takes guts. Wise couples are those who are open to trying out every possible solution that can help improve their marriage, even those methods that are less than conventional.

You can't change your partner by getting married and you can't change your marriage by changing your partner.

A lot of people make the mistake of assuming that marriage will change their partner only to become bitterly disappointed when they finally learn the truth. When you marry someone, you take them for who they are right now and not for who you want them to be in the future. It's your job to determine *before* marriage if there's something about your future husband/wife that you don't think you can live with. After marriage, even small attempts to change your partner may feel as though you are nagging him. Worse, it makes your spouse feel as though he is not good enough for you.

If you think that by "fixing" your partner, you are somehow going to fix your marriage, think again. The only person whom you can actually change in your marriage is yourself.

Give more.

Think of marriage as a savings account. Your deposits should always be more than your withdrawals. For each error that you commit, you need to make up for it ten times more. The ratio of positive to negative experiences in your marriage should be 5:1. That is, for every bad experience that you have, make five more positive experiences to balance it out. For every criticism that you make, give five encouraging statements to your spouse.

Problems are not always meant to be solved.

Not every complication has a fixed answer and there isn't always a correct way to handle a marriage issue. It's all about a matter of finding what's *right for the both of you.* More often, the secret is simply learning how to manage the problems in the marriage… how to live with them and how to cope with them as they arise, while maintaining the love and respect that you have for each other.

Respect begets respect.

In marriage, you become one. As such, to show disrespect to your partner would be to disrespect yourself. Respect in marriage is meant to be mutual. It is also meant to be constant. If you lose respect to your partner even on an occasional basis, you send a message that he is not worth valuing. This is not something which cannot and will not easily be forgotten by the injured party. You need to treat your husband/wife the exact same way that you'd want to be treated.

Consistency is the key.

In order for trust to grow, your actions should always be congruent with your words. When you get married, apart from your individual philosophies, you also develop values as a couple. Strive to act in coordination with those values. Another thing you should be consistent about is the support that you provide to your spouse. Show your significant other that you love him through tough times just as you would during the good times. Doing so will provide your partner with a sense of security and stability that's essential in a marriage.

Make decisions together.

When you're married, everything that you do will affect your partner in one way or another; thus, it is important that for each action that you take, you also take your partner's feelings and thoughts into consideration. You need to include your spouse in every decision-making opportunity about matters that will affect you as a couple. Never impose your opinion on your significant other.

It doesn't matter whether one of you has a better financial position or a higher educational attainment, both of you should have an equal say in all matters that concern the two of you. Remember that when you enter matrimony, you do it as two equal individuals who wish to become one. Whatever happens to your marriage, you are both equally responsible for it.

A crisis does not signify the death of a marriage.

Understand that the greatest marriages are not always those that have sailed smoothly. These are those that have gone through tempests and have survived together to tell about it.

Chapter 2 - What are the Top Causes of Divorce? How Do We Prevent Them?

Getting hitched for all the wrong reasons

This may range from unplanned pregnancies to marrying someone for money. Couples who treat marriage as though it's a solution to a problem are more likely to get divorced. Research also reveals that a great number of divorcees have been pressured into tying the knot because they believed that it was something they *had to do* at that point in their lives. The solution here is to pay no heed to the tick-tocking biological clock or to the click-clacking tongues of peers or elder relatives. Get married when you're good and ready, but more than that, get married because you and your partner love each other and want to spend the rest of your lives together.

Ineffective communication

Each time you neglect to share your feelings with each other, you create a distance that's difficult to bridge. Maintain open lines of communication. Set aside some time at the end of the day to really talk to each other about how you're feeling and what you're thinking. Don't do it over dinner or in front of the television. Don't wait until one of you is dying to hit the sack. In fact, don't attempt to discuss important matters when your spouse is physically or mentally exhausted.

Money matters

Money can influence marriage in 2 ways: it can make your life better, or it can make your life a living hell. Incompatibility in the financial area can threaten a marriage like no other. Married couples who are experiencing financial difficulties undergo a great deal of stress, which causes them to argue constantly. Many newlyweds make the mistake of acquiring too much debt early on in their marriage. They use up all their resources to pay for an expensive wedding, a bigger house, a honeymoon that they can't afford, etc.

When a sudden change in financial circumstances occurs, this threatens the harmony in the home. When one of you is unable to adjust to the new lifestyle, divorce may end up being the only possible solution in sight. Still, it doesn't even matter if your combined income can provide you with more than enough to live by. There will always be conflicts between the spendthrift and the saver, which will unavoidably create a strain in the relationship.

It's impossible to live with someone who constantly criticizes how you spend your money just as it's unbearable to live under the same roof with someone who keeps spending money that they think ought to be set aside. Ideally, these are issues that should have been addressed before getting hitched but if such isn't the case, then it would be wise to open up the issue *now*.

Moreover, when it comes to meeting expenses, couples should have a clear understanding as to who will take care of which. To avoid fighting and blaming each other, talk about whose responsibility it is to pay the bills, buy the groceries, pay for the kids' education, etc. Always practice fairness in dividing financial responsibilities.

Unmet expectations

When someone in the marriage is unhappy, his tendency would be to force the other to change so he can be happy again. Thus, the complaining, criticizing, nagging, and blaming part begins. Each time you ask your spouse to change, you are asking him to sacrifice his comfort for the sake of your own. One thing that you must understand is that it's you and you alone who is responsible for your own happiness.

The feeling that marriage constrains you

Some people feel like their marriage is holding them back from grabbing opportunities and achieving their dreams. The regret and resentment that follows is not always intentional. To prevent this, build each other up. Meet each other's needs while supporting each other's career decisions. Discuss and work on your common goals as a couple, but at the same time, listen to your significant other when he talks about his individual goals. You don't have to be an expert in his field; you just need to show interest in his work. More importantly, give your partner the time that he needs to fulfill his dreams or passions. Likewise, use this as an opportunity to work towards your own aspirations.

Forgetting who you are as a person and as a couple

Once you get married and assume the role of husband/wife, more roles inevitably follow. Soon, you find that you've taken the role of provider/homemaker, father/mother, head of the household, etc. The problem with this is that you end up forgetting that before you were all these things, you were a couple first. It comes to a point where you can't even remember why you got married first place. All you're sure of is that you have kids and that you share a house and so you need to stick with each other.

Here's another problem: When people get married, they usually let go of their single ways. This is good and somewhat expected *but* if you choose to let go of *everything* that connects you to your single life, you end up forgetting who you are as a person. It reaches a point where you can't even have fun on your own. You can't even recall the stuff that you used to like without getting it mixed up with the things that your spouse likes.

When you lose your sense of identity, you become less desirable to your partner. You end up reminding your significant other too much of himself. You've grown too familiar and there's just not enough mystery to excite each other anymore.

One way to fix this would be to schedule regular date nights where you can get in touch with who you are as a couple. During these dates, momentarily forget about your other responsibilities and roles and just be each other's lover. Look deep into one another and recall the qualities that attracted you to each other.

When intimacy vanishes

Women generally need romance in order to be open to sex. Likewise, men usually need sex in order to be open to romance. At the beginning of the marriage, perhaps both parties won't have much trouble meeting each other's needs, but somewhere along the way, some things will unavoidably change. People get old, jobs grow more demanding, kids require attention, someone will get ill, etc.

If she pulls back in the sex department, he pulls back in the romance department and vice versa. Before you know it, you're having less sex than you used to. Then, you realize that you're not having any at all! Sooner or later, the couples realize that they've become less and less like husband and wife and more and more like roommates. One or both of them will end up feeling unappreciated and unloved.

To prevent this, stay in touch... like, literally. Hold, kiss and caress each other frequently. While you may not be able to have sex as often as you used to, hello kisses and goodbye hugs and spontaneous affectionate touching will prevent you from turning into strangers.

Incompatibility

Some couples start off really strong, sharing the same passions, goals, values and visions of success earlier in their marriage. However, people inevitably change as they grow older. The sad thing is when they grow apart. When couples are incompatible, one or both are likely to end up seeking interaction with someone who understands them better; hence, leading the way to infidelity and extramarital relations. Prevent this by exploring new things together. It can be a new hobby, a new place, a new sex position.

Each time you discover something new and enjoy it, you feel a certain rush and a deeper bond with the person whom you did it with. Furthermore, doing things for the first time together makes you vulnerable to your partner; thus, deepening your intimacy. Grow together by constantly talking about your shared interests and priorities and finding ways on how to accomplish them together.

When you're unable to resolve conflicts effectively

It's normal for couples to disagree from time to time. The secret is to establish ground rules so that you and your partner will still feel respected even when you are arguing. Another major cause of divorce is abuse, be it verbal or physical. This problem often exists when one or both is suffering from any form of addiction or personality disorder such as narcissistic personality disorder or codependency. Such relationships are not healthy and may require intervention from a third party whom the couple trusts.

Chapter 3 – Ten Steps to Prevent a Divorce

Divorce is painful, but can be prevented if you think proactively. Many times couples for years ignore the obvious signs that a relationship is going downhill and therefore avoid communicating with each other.

Here are some steps to prevent the divorce:

Don't play victim

If you tell your spouse "how could you do this to me?"-that doesn't help. It only makes you fell more depressed about being with your spouse. Instead, remind yourself of the great things you have done in the marriage. Constantly thinking of yourself as the victim is a recipe for disaster because it leads to negativity, self-doubt, and low energy in a marriage. Therefore-a poor marriage and likely a divorce. Don't let this happen.

Define where you need to improve

Think back and take note of everything negative that you spouse has said to you. Bring this list to your spouse and talk it over with them. Be sure that you were self aware in compiling this list and that you didn't leave anything out.

Ask yourself why you made the mistakes you did. Think back to the origin of every mistake. If you don't know why you consistently made mistakes-then you won't know how to fix them.

Come up with an action plan on how you will fix those mistakes. Research on the internet or read self-help books if necessary to give you some good ideas on how to break those bad habits (I recommend *The Power of Habit* by Charles Duhigg for this). Be sure to keep that list with you so you can focus on fixing your bad habits.

Take care of yourself

Just because you're married doesn't mean that you should stop shaving your pubes, gain lots of weight, and not look presentable anymore. You and your partner should be sexy to each other! Continue to exercise and eat well. For women-continue to wear slutty lingerie every now and then. It is important that the two of you remain intimate. Especially about sex! Try to have sex at least 3-4 times a week.

For more information on sex-check out my book "Marriage and Sex" and my many other books regarding sex. Sex is awesome and a lot of fun. Don't kid yourself out of sex! Be unapologetically raunchy about what you want out of your sex life with your partner.

Kiss and make up

This might be the hardest part. Talk each other through calmly about both what each of you does well but also where each of you can improve. The hardest part is to be honest with each other.

Write down a number of times each of you were bitter and angry at each other. Look for the misunderstandings and misperceptions.

Apologize for each problem you caused. Learn from your mistakes so these don't happen again. Talk each other through how you both, not just one of you, will aim to avoid these problems in the future.

Believe that you deserve to be loved

Give yourself a pat on the back each day. Know that you are doing your best and that you deserve to be loved. If you don't believe that and continue to feel sorry for yourself, nothing will ever improve. This level of defeating self-doubt will do you no good. Sincerely believe that you are doing your best.

Study relationship material

By picking up this book, you are automatically moving in the right direction. Being proactive about relationship issues and studying relationship books is critical. It helps you learn from other people's mistakes so you don't have to make them all yourself. This simple hack alone can do vast amounts for your relationship health.

Connect with your partner everyday

You don't have to spend large amounts of time with your partner everyday. In fact, in a lot of ways that can be detrimental to your relationship. Too much time together can cause you both to get bored of each other.

However, it is important to spend quality time together every single day. Even if it is just a simple 30-minute walk together down the neighborhood, or a 15-minute sex session. The important thing is to make sure that you two are having some intimate time together each day.

Find some great hobbies to do together, whether they be cooking, bowling, golfing, etc. Having shared interests, and even better-working towards something together

Compliment your spouse everyday

This is huge. This is very simple advice-but few follow it. Most couples only tell each other what they are doing wrong. This is a great way to lift your partner's spirits each day. This one simple tip alone may make the difference between an average marriage and a great marriage. Doing this everyday pays huge dividends down the road, as it is a way of reminding your spouse that you still love each other.

Love your partner in the way he or she wants to be loved

Loving your partner the way you want to be loved might not be as meaningful as loving your partner the way they want to be loved. Some things that inspire you may not interest them. Be sure you take their interests and desires to heart when you give them a gift or show love. For example, if your partner does not like to receive chocolates-do not give them chocolates as a surprise. Know what your partner likes and doesn't like. By making silly mistakes like this-it communicates that you don't know your partner as well as you should.

Have strong standards for your marriage and stick to them

One of the best ways to prevent divorce in the first place is to have a solid foundation for your marriage in the first place. Define your vision for your marriage, where you want it to go and what you will not tolerate. Defining these terms and revisiting them at least once a month is a simple "Marriage Hack" that can lead the two of you eliminate problems long before they happen.

This works because frequently reviewing your marriage terms and terms with each other allows you and your spouse to tell each other what each of you is doing wrong and what each of you needs to improve upon without too much repeated mistakes.

Conclusion

I hope this book was able to help you learn how to reconnect with your significant other and use effective communication techniques to resolve marital conflicts.

The next step is to apply these marriage tips and communication strategies to help your marriage remain strong in the midst of a divorce culture. Remember, marriage ends when you've stopped loving each other, not because you've stumbled upon a crisis or two.

Finally, if you enjoyed this book, please take the time to share your thoughts and post a review on Amazon. It'd be greatly appreciated!

Thank you and good luck!

Marriage 101

How to Have a Long-lasting, Happy and Intimate Marriage!

are for clarifying purposes only and are the owned by the owners themselves, not affiliated with this document.

Check Out My Other Books!

Thanks for downloading my book! I am a firm believer that in order to have a fulfilling family life-one must be properly prepared and understand the fundamentals of relationships, how to be a good parent, and live an exciting and adventurous sex life. As you can see, I have written a series of multiple books on marriage, sex, and parenting. If you are looking to learn more about how to improve your marriage, sex and dating life, family life, etc.-please check out my other books! Simply click on the links below or search the titles below to check them out.

Parenting:

Parenting 101: 20 strategies to follow to raise well-behaved children

Raising Your Kids: Time Management for Parents for Stress-Free Parenting

Sex (General):

Sex Positions: Your Guide to the 50 Best Sex Positions for a sexy marriage!

Tantra Sex: The Beginner's Guide to 25 Tantra Techniques

Tantric Massage: Your Guide to the Best 30 Tantric Massage Techniques

BDSM Positions: The Beginner's Guide to 30 BDSM Techniques

Sex: Spice Up Your Sex Life! How to be maintain an awesome sex life with your partner and live your wildest sexual fantasies!

Sex Games: 35 Naughty Sex Games to make your Sex Life Hot!

Sex For Women:

Sexting: Sexting Tips for Women: 100 tips to turn him on!

Sex Positions for Women: The Ultimate Guide to the 50 Best Techniques to Turn Your Man On!

Talk Dirty: How to talk to get your man aroused and in the mood for sex!

Sex: The Hottest Tips for Better Orgasms!

Sex for Men:

Sex Positions for Men: The Ultimate Guide to the 50 Best Techniques to Turn Her On!

Dirty Talk: Talking Dirty for Men: 200 Examples to Get Your Girl Aroused and in the Mood for Sex!

Sex: Make her beg for more and be the best she's ever been with in bed!

Marriage:

Marriage and Sex: Why sex matters to keep romance alive!

Marriage for Women: Your Guide to a Happy, Fulfilling, Intimate Marriage!

Marriage for Men: How to be a good husband and have a happy, fulfilling, intimate marriage!

Marriage 101: How to have a long-lasting, happy and intimate marriage!

Wedding Planning: The Ultimate Guide to Budgeting and Planning your Wedding!

Marriage Communication: Your Guide to constructive praise, criticism, and communication for a happy, long-lasting marriage!

Divorce: Ten Steps to Preventing a Divorce and Save Your Marriage

Dating:

Tinder Dating: Your Guide to Creating a Strong Tinder Profile, Getting a First Date, and Being Confident!

Contents

Introduction

I want to thank you and congratulate you for downloading the book, *"Marriage 101: How to Have a Long-Lasting, Happy and Intimate Marriage!"*

This book contains proven steps and strategies on how to apply the fundamentals of building a strong marriage, avoid the common causes of divorce, reignite the spark in your relationship, and develop effective communication techniques that can save your marriage.

Marriage is defined as a process where two individuals solidify their union, but in this society where divorce cases have continuously increased in number, the words "official" and "permanent" don't seem to mean as much as they used to. Are you really ready to accept that marriage is a dying institution? Through this book, you'll learn how to prevent your marriage from going down the divorce path.

Marriage is not for wimps. A marriage is truly over only when two people have ceased to love each other and not because they've encountered a crisis or two. Conflicts are normal in marriages. They can either ruin a marriage or make it stronger. However, it's not the nature of the problem that determines the kind of impact it'll have on your relationship. It's the way through which you handle the problem together, as a couple.

Through this book, you will learn practical strategies on how to resolve marital conflict effectively without having to fight. Find out how you can argue your way productively towards a solution.

A successful marriage is made up of a bunch of routines. It's what makes everything function and fit together. However, when routine finds its way into the bedroom, there can be no faster way to kill passion. Through these pages, you'll find tips on how to rekindle the fire in the hearth *and* between the sheets.

Thanks again for downloading this book, I hope you enjoy it!

Chapter 1 - What are the Fundamentals of a Strong Marriage?

Don't make promises you can't keep.

Marriages are based on promises right from the moment the couples say their vows. Therefore, you can't blame your spouse if he/she has developed certain expectations. When people are in love, they're ready to promise just about anything. However, failure to turn promises into reality can easily lead to frustration, mistrust and resentment. Keep it real. You don't have to promise him/her the moon and the stars. Instead, offer your spouse whatever you can give and whatever you're willing to give. Before making a promise to your partner, ask yourself: will I be able to keep my word when things go smoothly *and* when things go bad?

Happiness is something that you create.

Most couples make the mistake of thinking that happiness is a byproduct of marriage. In a way, it is, but here's the catch - you have to make it yourself. Happiness is something that you strive to achieve on a daily basis. It depends on your daily words, actions and choices. Successful married couples are able to learn to *intentionally* draw in happiness to their marriage by creating one beautiful memory after another. This entails effort, patience, understanding, openness and sharing. But more than that, they *do* things that can help bring happiness back into the marriage when the inevitable realities of life try to take that happiness away.

Love is not just a noun. It's also a verb.

At first, marriage creates this feel-good sensation. Newlywed couples live inside this bubble where everything seems possible as long as they're in love and together, but the thing is, love is not just a feeling. It's all about what you do when that bubble is punctured and you and your spouse are exposed to the realities of married life.

Get rid of "the grass is greener" mentality.

Quit entertaining thoughts like "Maybe I'll be happier with someone else." Or "Maybe I should've married my high school sweetheart instead..." etc. When your marriage is going through a rough patch, it's tempting to wonder about what-might-have-beens. As much as possible, you'd like to think that it's not your fault that your marriage is not up to fairy-tale standards. However, successful married couples have learned to understand that the grass is always greenest wherever you take care of it; thus, they invest time and energy into improving themselves and their marriage.

Doing the same old things lead to the same old results.

Smart couples understand the importance of exploring various approaches to address a problem. They don't make the mistake of applying the same old solution that has failed them in the past. They know that doing so will only lead to further disappointment and hopelessness. Sometimes, a small change in attitude or a mere modification of action can make a tremendous difference. Furthermore, fixing marriage issues takes guts. Wise couples are those who are open to trying out every possible solution that can help improve their marriage, even those methods that are less than conventional.

You can't change your partner by getting married and you can't change your marriage by changing your partner.

A lot of people make the mistake of assuming that marriage will change their partner only to become bitterly disappointed when they finally learn the truth. When you marry someone, you take them for who they are right now and not for who you want them to be in the future. It's your job to determine *before* marriage if there's something about your future husband/wife that you don't think you can live with. After marriage, even small attempts to change your partner may feel as though you are nagging him. Worse, it makes your spouse feel as though he is not good enough for you.

If you think that by "fixing" your partner, you are somehow going to fix your marriage, think again. The only person whom you can actually change in your marriage is yourself.

Give more.

Think of marriage as a savings account. Your deposits should always be more than your withdrawals. For each error that you commit, you need to make up for it ten times more. The ratio of positive to negative experiences in your marriage should be 5:1. That is, for every bad experience that you have, make five more positive experiences to balance it out. For every criticism that you make, give five encouraging statements to your spouse.

Problems are not always meant to be solved.

Not every complication has a fixed answer and there isn't always a correct way to handle a marriage issue. It's all about a matter of finding what's *right for the both of you*. More often, the secret is simply learning how to manage the problems in the marriage... how to live with them and how to cope with them as they arise, while maintaining the love and respect that you have for each other.

Respect begets respect.

In marriage, you become one. As such, to show disrespect to your partner would be to disrespect yourself. Respect in marriage is meant to be mutual. It is also meant to be constant. If you lose respect to your partner even on an occasional basis, you send a message that he is not worth valuing. This is not something which cannot and will not easily be forgotten by the injured party. You need to treat your husband/wife the exact same way that you'd want to be treated.

Consistency is the key.

In order for trust to grow, your actions should always be congruent with your words. When you get married, apart from your individual philosophies, you also develop values as a couple. Strive to act in coordination with those values. Another thing you should be consistent about is the support that you provide to your spouse. Show your significant other that you love him through tough times just as you would during the good times. Doing so will provide your partner with a sense of security and stability that's essential in a marriage.

Make decisions together.

When you're married, everything that you do will affect your partner in one way or another; thus, it is important that for each action that you take, you also take your partner's feelings and thoughts into consideration. You need to include your spouse in every decision-making opportunity about matters that will affect you as a couple. Never impose your opinion on your significant other.

It doesn't matter whether one of you has a better financial position or a higher educational attainment, both of you should have an equal say in all matters that concern the two of you. Remember that when you enter matrimony, you do it as two equal individuals who wish to become one. Whatever happens to your marriage, you are both equally responsible for it.

A crisis does not signify the death of a marriage.

Understand that the greatest marriages are not always those that have sailed smoothly. These are those that have gone through tempests and have survived together to tell about it.

Chapter 2 - What are the Top Causes of Divorce? How Do We Prevent Them?

Getting hitched for all the wrong reasons

This may range from unplanned pregnancies to marrying someone for money. Couples who treat marriage as though it's a solution to a problem are more likely to get divorced. Research also reveals that a great number of divorcees have been pressured into tying the knot because they believed that it was something they *had to do* at that point in their lives. The solution here is to pay no heed to the tick-tocking biological clock or to the click-clacking tongues of peers or elder relatives. Get married when you're good and ready, but more than that, get married because you and your partner love each other and want to spend the rest of your lives together.

Ineffective communication

Each time you neglect to share your feelings with each other, you create a distance that's difficult to bridge. Maintain open lines of communication. Set aside some time at the end of the day to really talk to each other about how you're feeling and what you're thinking. Don't do it over dinner or in front of the television. Don't wait until one of you is dying to hit the sack. In fact, don't attempt to discuss important matters when your spouse is physically or mentally exhausted.

Money matters

Money can influence marriage in 2 ways: it can make your life better, or it can make your life a living hell. Incompatibility in the financial area can threaten a marriage like no other. Married couples who are experiencing financial difficulties undergo a great deal of stress, which causes them to argue constantly. Many newlyweds make the mistake of acquiring too much debt early on in their marriage. They use up all their resources to pay for an expensive wedding, a bigger house, a honeymoon that they can't afford, etc.

When a sudden change in financial circumstances occurs, this threatens the harmony in the home. When one of you is unable to adjust to the new lifestyle, divorce may end up being the only possible solution in sight. Still, it doesn't even matter if your combined income can provide you with more than enough to live by. There will always be conflicts between the spendthrift and the saver, which will unavoidably create a strain in the relationship.

It's impossible to live with someone who constantly criticizes how you spend your money just as it's unbearable to live under the same roof with someone who keeps spending money that they think ought to be set aside. Ideally, these are issues that should have been addressed before getting hitched but if such isn't the case, then it would be wise to open up the issue *now*.

Moreover, when it comes to meeting expenses, couples should have a clear understanding as to who will take care of which. To avoid fighting and blaming each other, talk about whose responsibility it is to pay the bills, buy the groceries, pay for the kids' education, etc. Always practice fairness in dividing financial responsibilities.

Unmet expectations

When someone in the marriage is unhappy, his tendency would be to force the other to change so he can be happy again. Thus, the complaining, criticizing, nagging, and blaming part begins. Each time you ask your spouse to change, you are asking him to sacrifice his comfort for the sake of your own. One thing that you must understand is that it's you and you alone who is responsible for your own happiness.

The feeling that marriage constrains you

Some people feel like their marriage is holding them back from grabbing opportunities and achieving their dreams. The regret and resentment that follows is not always intentional. To prevent this, build each other up. Meet each other's needs while supporting each other's career decisions. Discuss and work on your common goals as a couple, but at the same time, listen to your significant other when he talks about his individual goals. You don't have to be an expert in his field; you just need to show interest in his work. More importantly, give your partner the time that he needs to fulfill his dreams or passions. Likewise, use this as an opportunity to work towards your own aspirations.

Forgetting who you are as a person and as a couple

Once you get married and assume the role of husband/wife, more roles inevitably follow. Soon, you find that you've taken the role of provider/homemaker, father/mother, head of the household, etc. The problem with this is that you end up forgetting that before you were all these things, you were a couple first. It comes to a point where you can't even remember why you got married first place. All you're sure of is that you have kids and that you share a house and so you need to stick with each other.

Here's another problem: When people get married, they usually let go of their single ways. This is good and somewhat expected *but* if you choose to let go of *everything* that connects you to your single life, you end up forgetting who you are as a person. It reaches a point where you can't even have fun on your own. You can't even recall the stuff that you used to like without getting it mixed up with the things that your spouse likes.

When you lose your sense of identity, you become less desirable to your partner. You end up reminding your significant other too much of himself. You've grown too familiar and there's just not enough mystery to excite each other anymore.

One way to fix this would be to schedule regular date nights where you can get in touch with who you are as a couple. During these dates, momentarily forget about your other responsibilities and roles and just be each other's lover. Look deep into one another and recall the qualities that attracted you to each other.

When intimacy vanishes

Women generally need romance in order to be open to sex. Likewise, men usually need sex in order to be open to romance. At the beginning of the marriage, perhaps both parties won't have much trouble meeting each other's needs, but somewhere along the way, some things will unavoidably change. People get old, jobs grow more demanding, kids require attention, someone will get ill, etc.

If she pulls back in the sex department, he pulls back in the romance department and vice versa. Before you know it, you're having less sex than you used to. Then, you realize that you're not having any at all! Sooner or later, the couples realize that they've become less and less like husband and wife and more and more like roommates. One or both of them will end up feeling unappreciated and unloved.

To prevent this, stay in touch... like, literally. Hold, kiss and caress each other frequently. While you may not be able to have sex as often as you used to, hello kisses and goodbye hugs and spontaneous affectionate touching will prevent you from turning into strangers.

Incompatibility

Some couples start off really strong, sharing the same passions, goals, values and visions of success earlier in their marriage. However, people inevitably change as they grow older. The sad thing is when they grow apart. When couples are incompatible, one or both are likely to end up seeking interaction with someone who understands them better; hence, leading the way to infidelity and extramarital relations. Prevent this by exploring new things together. It can be a new hobby, a new place, a new sex position.

Each time you discover something new and enjoy it, you feel a certain rush and a deeper bond with the person whom you did it with. Furthermore, doing things for the first time together makes you vulnerable to your partner; thus, deepening your intimacy. Grow together by constantly talking about your shared interests and priorities and finding ways on how to accomplish them together.

When you're unable to resolve conflicts effectively

It's normal for couples to disagree from time to time. The secret is to establish ground rules so that you and your partner will still feel respected even when you are arguing. Another major cause of divorce is abuse, be it verbal or physical. This problem often exists when one or both is suffering from any form of addiction or personality disorder such as narcissistic personality disorder or codependency. Such relationships are not healthy and may require intervention from a third party whom the couple trusts.

Chapter 3 - How Do We Reignite the Spark in Our Marriage and Reconnect with Each Other?

Tell each other "I love you" more often.

This sounds like a really simple advice, but it works like a charm. Couples who have been together for so long tend to discount the importance of kind words like "Please" and "Thank you."

Have more sex.

Here's another no-brainer, but here's the thing, couples who have been married for several years experience a decrease in their libido. The causes may range from physical exhaustion to hormonal changes to side effects of prescription medication. In one way or another, these causes are usually connected with the natural process of growing old. One thing you can do to be able to have sex more often is to stay fit together. Eat healthy, rehydrate, perform regular exercise, etc. Avoid negative habits that can have a diminishing effect on your libido like drinking too much alcohol.

Naturally, a lot of things will try to get in the way like work, housework, kids, etc. The solution would be to schedule your sexy time. Determine which night of the week it would be most convenient to leave your kids at grandma's and grandpa's. If this isn't an option, talk with your married friends who also have kids and then help each other out. Or you can always hire a sitter then check in at a motel. There are so many possible options if you're really determined to reconnect with each other on a physical and emotional level.

If it's not possible for you to have sex at the moment, there's no earthly reason why you can't let your partner know that you're thinking about doing it with him. Let your spouse know through words or through touch that you're eagerly looking forward to the next time that you'll make love. Send each other sexy text messages and communicate your passion through your eyes while having dinner. This will help build the anticipation so that the next time you make love, it'll feel fantastic.

If you want to tune in to each other, then you need to tune out to technology.

So, do you want to sleep with your spouse or do you want to sleep with your phone? Use your bedroom only when you want to: a) sleep and b) make love. An ideal set-up would be to transform your bedroom into your very own carnal temple. Get rid of anything that will remind you of the routines and responsibilities of daily life. (ex. bills, laundry lists, papers from work, etc.) Instead, furnish your bedroom so that it will encourage passion. Use dim lighting, light scented candles, and play soft music.

Don't bring your gadgets into the bedroom and get rid of the television in your boudoir or you'll get lost in the world of social media and the sports channel and trashy talk shows. Each time you mindlessly surf through the net, you're losing an opportunity to spend some precious alone time with your spouse. (And by alone time, that doesn't mean surfing the web while sitting side by side in bed!)

Constantly express your appreciation throughout the day.

This can be as simple as uttering a kind word or sending a sweet text message. If you can, look into your significant other's eyes and tell him just how great he is and how he makes your life so much better. Be generous with your compliments. Boost your spouse's self-confidence by telling him how lovely or smart or sexy he is at every opportunity that you can get. That said, make sure that your comments are heartfelt. This means that each time you look at your spouse, you have to intentionally look for all the wonderful traits that he possesses.

Be a lover, not a critic.

As mentioned in the previous chapter, keeping date nights alive is essential to a successful marriage. Another important thing to remember is that it would be impossible to reconnect and rekindle your passion if you're constantly looking for the negative stuff. Nothing kills the mood like complaining about the horribly directed movie or the overcooked main course.

Each time you do this, you make your husband/wife feel as though you are actually complaining about his/her company. When spouse feels like he has failed you, he is unlikely to exert more effort to please you. Why should they, when it's almost impossible to meet your expectations? To fix this, focus on the positive aspects of your time together like how nice the restaurant's ambience is or how great he looks.

Make an effort to look good.

Look into the mirror and ask yourself this: Would *you* even want to be married to *you*? A better alternative to growing old together would be to grow old *gracefully* together. It can be a scary thing for both parties to wake up one morning, see the person beside them and think: "Is this really the same man/woman that I married?"

Don't wait 'til the physical attraction starts to wane to make your move. A tragic truth about marriage and divorce is that often, the loss of physical interest between spouses is actually the real cause of separation and is merely aggravated by all the other marital problems that have accumulated throughout the years.

As much as possible, you'd have to remind your spouse that you're still the same person that he had been so crazy in love and "in lust" with. Improving yourself physically will not only boost your self-esteem and get rid of insecurities and jealousies; it will also give your spouse more reason to be proud that you're his; hence, to take care of your body is to take care of your marriage.

Use the years to your advantage.

Sex between long married couples is a special thing because you've been together long enough to understand each other's bodies. You're able to decode the meaning of each look, each gesture and each sound. Furthermore, you've gotten past the shyness that's typical in the dating stage. Therefore, sex is supposed to be more pleasurable, more spontaneous, and ultimately more meaningful. So why isn't that the case? That's because you've fallen into a lovemaking routine and when sex falls into a predictable pattern, one or both of the married couple end up fantasizing (consciously or subconsciously) about doing it with someone with a little more mystery and a little more surprise.

To prevent thoughts of infidelity from creeping into your marriage, sit down together and have intimate conversations about your deepest fantasies. Make a list of each other's carnal suggestions and compromise on which one you're willing to try. Never say "Never." to your partner. Instead, say "We'll see." Make sure that this is a fair give and take thing.

Chapter 4 - How Do We Communicate More Effectively with Each Other?

Talk and Touch

Each time you and your partner engage in mundane dialogue, move a little closer. Rest your head on your spouse's shoulder, hold each other's hands, or caress each other's back. This physical intimacy will help provide you with a sense of comfort which will, in turn, encourage a more open conversation. Soon, you'll be talking about more intimate and meaningful topics.

Listen actively.

This sounds awfully simple but it's surprisingly difficult for some couples to really follow. Listening is a lot different from hearing. It's about momentarily putting aside your own point in order to allow your spouse the opportunity to get his point across. More than that, it's about being open to the possibility that you may be wrong and your husband/wife may be right. Now, how many people can actually do that when they're knee deep in an argument?

Most of the time, your tendency is to keep talking so you can make sure that you'll be heard. But here's the thing, when you don't allow your spouse to verbalize his thoughts, he will be so preoccupied with them that in the end, you're still unlikely to be heard. Instead of trying to formulate hot rejoinders in your head, focus your attention to what your other half is trying to say.

Validate.

When listening, don't just use your ears. Use your eyes and your whole body to show your partner that you really are listening to him. Face each other while talking. Mind your body language. Crossed arms suggest defensiveness. Make eye contact to show that you're interested in your other half's opinion. A subtle frown or a slight raise of an eyebrow can send strong and sometimes wrong messages. To show that you're really into the conversation, utilize bridge phrases like: "How did you feel about that?" and "What are you planning to do now?"

Keep your emotions in check when discussing important issues that require decision-making.

Hot topics like money, children and the future should not be discussed when one of you is feeling emotionally vulnerable. You're probably thinking: *How can I talk about these things and not get emotional?* The thing is you both need to be rational in order to fully see the consequences that accompany each decision.

Furthermore, you need to control your reactions. Remember that you can't take back hurtful words and the wounds that they create tend to leave very deep scars. Choose your words well. They need to be straightforward, sincere and sensitive. Avoid useless responses like storming out of the room mid-conversation or cutting your partner off while he is speaking.

Make use of introductions.

Refrain from blurting out sensitive questions or messages. Instead, break it to your significant other gently with a thoughtful preamble. For instance, instead of saying: "So, are you fine about me going on a trip or not?", say: "Hey, hubby, I'm not sure I understood your response about my weekend plans with the girls. When would be a nice time to talk about it some more?"

Develop empathy for each other.

Sure, it's not that easy to put your feelings aside if you're angry, tired, or feeling as though your needs are not being met, but place yourself in your spouse's shoes. How would you feel like if you have the same workload or health condition or financial responsibilities? How would you feel if you suddenly had to take on his role? Think about how your actions and your words may affect your other half. Each time you feel the urge to criticize, think of how you will feel like if you heard the same words coming from your husband/wife?

Use mirroring.

When you feel like you didn't really comprehend what your significant other was trying to tell you, the last thing that you'd want him to think is that you weren't paying attention. This is where the mirroring technique can be useful.

Example: "I feel stressed out and awkward each time your parents come to visit."

Mirror response: "What I hear is you prefer that they stay in a hotel whenever they come to the city. That way, they can be more comfortable while we can maintain our privacy. I can see why you would prefer that."

After voicing out your interpretation of his statement, wait for your other half to verify whether or not that was what he truly meant.

Chapter 5 - How Do We Argue Without Fighting?

Productive arguing does not involve shouting.

When you're discussing sensitive topics, the first thing that you need to do is to get yourself out of fight mode. Raising your voice won't guarantee that you'll be heard. In fact, heavy emotion can cloud the clarity of the situation.

Attack the issue, not each other.

Productive arguing mainly focuses on finding a solution to the problem. Some couples make the mistake of straying from the actual issue and end up digging up each other's past mistakes. This does nothing but add more problems and hurt each other's emotions. Keep things relevant and tackle one problem at a time. Whatever you do, do not resort to cursing each other or calling each other names.

As mentioned in the first chapter, respect in marriage should be mutual and consistent. It should be present even when you're deep in argument. Using a polite tone, ask your partner for an alternative solution to the issue. Then, carefully consider each other's suggestions.

Have a goal in mind before going into an argument.

For an argument to be productive, you need to know that it's worth having in the first place. What do you really want? What do you hope to achieve by getting into a discussion with your significant other? Be real about the issues that are truly bothering you. Tell it in a matter-of-fact manner and go straight to core problem instead of addressing its symptoms.

For instance, if your real problem is your husband's drinking, then don't keep complaining about how he comes home late at night or how he keeps spending time with his "good-for-nothing" friends. Tell your husband that you're concerned about his drinking behavior and how it may affect him and your marriage.

Argue so that you can finally agree on something.

Productive argument always ends in cooperation. Through the process, make sure that you identify points where you agree on. Once you've found a common ground, finding a solution will become a lot easier.

There's no winner in WIN-LOSE situations.

When it comes to marital arguments, your goal is not to win. Because the truth is, when one of you loses, you both lose. So forget about who's right or wrong. Instead, try to determine if what you're doing is working or not. If, after the argument, you end up being right after all, don't rub it into your spouse's face. Allow him to retreat with his dignity intact. Avoid blaming. Avoid shaming.

Furthermore, learn to recognize when you're being offered a truce. It's tempting to allow the argument to go on if you're starting to feel like you're "winning" but ask yourself: *"Do I want to win? Or do I want to stay married?"*

Be prepared to apologize whether or not you think you've done something wrong. Moreover, don't wait for your significant other to apologize first. When you do, this shows that you're more concerned about being right than about actually reconciling with your partner.

Specifically address a negative action instead of speaking about your spouse's behavior in general.

For instance, instead of accusing your spouse of being "lazy", cite specific instances when you felt like he hadn't been doing his part in the housework.

Correct approach: "Last night, when you didn't take out the garbage, it made me feel as though you're not taking your household responsibilities seriously."

Utilize "I" and "We" statements.

Refrain from using heavy "You" words like "You should", "You better", and "You don't". Instead, utilize "I" and "We" statements to get your message across in a non-threatening manner.

Example:

Instead of saying: "You don't listen to me.", say: "I feel like we should talk and listen to each other more often."

Begin and end each argument with an affirmation that you and your spouse care about each other.

Even while arguing, remind your other half that you love and trust him. Conflicts are normal in every marriage. Use them as opportunities to learn more about each other and to learn from each other.

Marriage for Men:

How to be a good husband and have a happy, fulfilling, intimate marriage!

Introduction

Are you a man having trouble reigniting the passion you once shared with your wife?

Are you a father having trouble balancing time with the kids and working full time?

Are you just a chap who needs some general marriage advice?

This book provides you with general knowledge on how to get your marriage blooming again, from communicating with your wife, getting the romance back on, to getting the passion back in the bedroom, as well as balancing your personal interests, your family life, and your work. In this book are helpful insights and tips in order for you to have a happy and long lasting marriage.

Chapter 1 - Communication in Marriage

"There is no more lovely, friendly, and charming relationship, communion or company than a good marriage."

– Martin Luther

Communication is important in any relationship and more so in a marriage. You have sworn to spend the rest of your life with your wife, to go through life and build a family with her. And to live the rest of your life happily with a woman, you need to know how to communicate with each other and share your thoughts and plans with each other intimately.

Communication can be a problem to many couples however, and your own personal differences are a big factor in this, but you also have to be conscious of the fact that men and women also have different ways of communicating, but in order to have a successful married life, you will have to get through these differences. In this chapter, you will find new ideas in communicating with your wife for a happier married life.

Communicate effectively

There are various ways of communicating with your wife, but not all of them are effective and being ineffective in communication can be a cause for a lot of arguments. You have to realize how men and women differ in their communication strategies and how the sexes tend to express their feelings.

Listening

Women have a tendency of wanting to talk about all sorts of things, and more so when they are stressed. They want to express themselves, and by expressing themselves, they tend to feel better about themselves and whatever it was that caused them to become stressed out. Men are not like this. When faced with a problem, men would rather fix it or find a solution rather than talk about how they feel. This is where some of the misunderstanding can come from. When women want to talk about certain problems, men can become a bit resistant to it. Men tend to feel responsible when they find their wife talking about problems that they have, or they tend to give out clear cut advice, which is never really what the wife is looking for. The wife simply wants to be heard and understood, to have a sympathetic ear turned to her, not solutions or explanations.

Scenes like this tend to play out poorly once things get heated. One of the more important things a man has to learn to get along well with his wife is to simply listen when your wife is upset. Sometimes, the simple act of listening is all your wife needs to feel better.

Feeling like you are somehow responsible for a problem and have to solve it for your wife when she starts talking about problems, this feeling of responsibility can keep you from listening effectively. You have to understand that your wife's way of coping with stress is by talking about it and all you really have to do for her is to listen. You don't have to say much, listening itself can make your wife feel understood and loved.

Talking it out

Another major difference between men and women is the fact that men generally don't want to talk about their problems. They tend to withdraw to their so-called "man caves", becoming withdrawn and quiet, sometimes even emotionally unavailable to their wives. Women, as stated earlier, tend to want to talk about problems to relieve stress, and they will tend to worry about their husbands who grow quiet or withdrawn and not wanting to talk. Women can even start demanding attention from their husbands when this happens, making the man all the more withdrawn.

A good rule for you when you feel stressed and need to "retreat" is to give your wife a head's up. Tell her you need time to yourself and that she shouldn't worry; you'll be out and about soon. Make your wife understand that you need time to yourself to sort through the stress you are going through. This will keep her from worrying or feeling unloved, and give you the time and space you need to get it together and emerge from your cave as the loving and sweet husband you always aim to be for your wife.

Settling arguments

When you find yourself falling into an argument, it would be wise to let your wife speak her mind. Here are some guidelines on how to settle arguments.

1. Try to validate her FEELINGS even though you may not agree with her point. When your wife says, "We never go out!" understand that what she is saying is "I want to go out with you tonight, I want us to have fun." Try to understand what she's feeling and give her validation for how she feels.

2. Stay calm. Men have a tendency of becoming impatient and blow up when you start on an argument, or even just walk away and refuse to speak. It is important to stay calm during arguments and talk it out calmly with your spouse.

3. Know when to give it up. Sometimes there are just arguments that aren't even worth it. There are arguments that are just driven by emotions, and if you stop and think about it, you and your wife aren't really arguing about anything. Know when to throw the towel

during your arguments is important to keep the peace in your marriage. You might draw blood in a battle that wasn't even worth it.

It is very important for you to communicate well with your wife, to listen well, and express yourself, even if you don't want to, so you can understand each other better. Communication is important to avoid arguments but it is also important in settling arguments and keeping your home life amiable and happy.

Chapter 2 - Keeping the Peace

"Happy is the man who finds a true friend, and far happier is he who finds that true friend in his wife"

-Franz Schubert

It is important to have a strong sense of satisfaction within the marriage for it to last long. You and your wife both have to feel appreciated, cherished, and respected within the relationship for you to be satisfied. Having one party feel unappreciated and ignored can cause great harm to the relationship and, without proper communication, you may be surprised that your partner is unhappy and wants to end the marriage. It is important that you and your wife both feel fulfillment and appreciation in the marriage for it to work.

Showing your appreciation

Giving credit where it is due

If you happen to be the only bread winner in the family, it might be easy to belittle your wife's hard work and think that she isn't "really" working, despite the fact that this is clearly untrue. You may think this because you leave the house and arrive and find everything exactly the way it was when you left, or you find your wife watching TV on the sofa, but what you don't realize is she may have spent the day cleaning and organizing all day, doing the laundry and cooking dinner. It is easy to forget that getting the house to look the way it does is actually a very difficult task and takes up a lot of time and effort on her part, which makes her more dependent on you to give her credit, as she does not have a boss or co-workers to tell her she had done a great job, nor does she get a pay-check every two weeks, she only has you to tell her she did a good job and appreciate her efforts. Thank your wife now and again, tell her you love her cooking and that she does everything just right. Show her some appreciation now and then and go out of your way to make her feel loved.

Praise your wife

Giving praise can give a big boost of confidence for your wife, and will surely give you brownie points on the romance category. Go out of your way to praise your wife, on how she keeps house, on how she helps raise your children, on her work, and even just on her beauty. Just stop for a moment and give time to praise your wife, at least once a day. Think of the good things you love about her and why you fell in love with her in the first place then tell her about it. It is important for a woman to know that they are loved and cherished, and complementing your wife can bring out the best in her. It is a very effective way of building up your wife and keeping your marriage harmonious.

Determine and share responsibilities equally

One of the main reasons behind fighting can be because you have a misunderstanding when it comes to responsibility. Find a way that you and your wife can have an understanding of each other's responsibility, this way you and your wife will have a clear road map on what needs to be done. Be willing to share the load, not just in taking responsibility but also in making decisions.

If you feel you need to, such as if you are both working, you can make a list of things that need to be done, and assign the tasks accordingly betwixt you.

Once you have divided the responsibilities, be supportive of each other. Remember that you are both just human and you both need support in your responsibilities and decisions.

Maintain realistic expectations

Having unreasonable and unrealistic expectations can be very unfair to your wife. You have to realize that she is human and can't do everything perfectly all the time. It would be very unfair to expect her to cook and clean and take of the kids and just smile at the end of the day. Mothers and wives get tired too, and they can end up burning dinner, and it is at these times that she needs you to be supportive rather than critical of her shortcomings.

Try to be forthcoming about it, tell her that these are what you expect from her, i.e. support, love, keep the houseclean, cook a good dinner, get the kids to bed, entertain guests, pay for the electric and water, etc. and you can talk about what her expectations are of you, and just bounce the ideas around until you reach an agreement, what you can reasonably expect from which she will do her best to achieve, and what she can expect from you, which you will do your best to achieve too, on your part. It is important that you both have an agreement on the responsibilities that you have in the household, rather than just assuming that this is what one and the other should do, and get frustrated because your (unspoken) expectation was not met.

It is important that both you and your wife find satisfaction in your marriage for it to last. You should both be considerate of each other and what the other's role is within the family dynamic. It is important that you both are aware of what you are supposed to do and what the other can be reasonably expected to do. Knowing your roles and playing them right brings in a lot of satisfaction into the marriage.

Chapter 3 - Balance Work and Family

"A happy marriage is a long conversation which always seems too short."

– Andre Marois

In this industrialized world, you can get caught up in earning a living that you tend to forget how to live life. You work hard every year, promising yourself that next year, you will go out on that summer vacation in a foreign tropical country with your family, but years can pass by without you realizing that you've broken your promise several times already. It is important that you manage to balance the time you give to your family as well as the time you spend at work. Earning a living to support your family is important, but you also have to take the time to enjoy your life and be surrounded by people who love you. This chapter will give some tips on how to balance out work and family to make sure you don't miss out on living life.

Spend quality time with your family

Leave your work where you work

This simply means that you shouldn't bring work home with you. Although this may seem difficult, you can try it out from time to time. Or at least give an hour or two each day just dedicated on your family instead of work. Your family needs a father and a husband there with them, and you can't truly be that if half of your mind is at work, or if you spend what little time you have for your family at your study mulling over profits or cash flow, you are not only short-changing your family, you are short changing yourself by doing this. You are not allowing yourself to get to know your family and enjoy their company.

Have dinner together

One effective way of having your family together is by having dinner together, gather up the family and sit around a table together. Don't eat at random time whenever you get hungry, come together for dinner and discuss your day. Although it may seem cliché, having dinner is a good way to get updated on your family and how everyone is. Your child might be having some troubles at school and it is important that you remain open and non-judgmental on whatever might be said. Welcome the confidence in a calm and open way, encourage your family to speak and don't get angry over the dinner table. This can be a very good bonding moment if you wield it wisely.

Schedule your time

Have vacation together

There is a time to immerse yourself in work and a time to enjoy vacation and spend quality time with your family. Use the vacation time you are allocated for vacation to spend time with your family and have fun. Having a memorable vacation can do great things for your family life and can ease any tensions you may have within the family, not to mention give you a break from the hustle and bustle of daily life.

Deliver on your promises to 'be there'

Whenever your kids have activities at school and they ask you to come, and you say yes, do the best you can to be there. As much as possible, keep your word. Your children have to know that they can rely on their father and that you are someone who will not disappoint them. Being a trustworthy father to your children will teach them how important it is for them to keep their word and will make it easier for them to trust others when they grow up.

Schedule your work around your promises as a father, not the other way around. Make time and be there for them when you promise that you will.

It is important that you do not lose track of your children and how they are growing up despite your work. It is important for your kids to know that they have a father they can trust and rely on, who's got their back and loves them, a father who goes out of his way just to spend some extra time with them and get to know them better. A baseball game once a month at the park or a swim at the beach may not take that much of your time, but it can mean the world to your children and affect how they grow up when they get older. It is wise that you invest your time on your kids and be gladdened by the fact that you can watch them grow up to be great individuals.

Chapter 4 - Keeping the Romance Alive

"A successful marriage requires falling in love many times, always with the same person."

- *Mignon McLaughlin*

For your to have a happy and lasting marriage, you have to step up your game and keep the romance alive. Years of marriage and having children can dampen the romance in your marriage, not to mention your bust schedules and stresses you may have to go through every day. You tend to lose track of the romance that once sparked your little love story and it can leave a dull taste in your marriage.

After years of marriage, it may be time for you to start stepping up your game and bring the romance back to your marriage with these simple tips.

Sweet Nothings can mean everything

You must remember saying sweet nothings to your wife when you were just courting her right? You might even have kept it up when you first got married, but what happened? Why did you stop? Where did all the sweetness go? You could forget to be romantic after a while, especially when you get too busy and tired or are preoccupied with the kids and earning a living for your family. But where does the romance go? It gets buried in a ton of worries, play times and bills, but you can still get it back. Doing and saying sweet nothings can give your married life the jump-start it needs.

Surprise your wife

Go out of your way to give your wife a sweet token at random times. Take her out to dinner out of the blue, or send her a bouquet of flowers when you're on your way to work, it doesn't have to be an expensive token or surprise, it just has to be meaningful to both of you. The more random it is, the sweeter it can be. Don't forget to send her a card that says thank you just because. A sweet and simple token of your love and appreciation for what your wife has done for you will go a long way in the romance department and ignite a few embers of romance that ha vied down.

Have a weekly or monthly date night

Although surprise is a great way to get the romance burning again, it is also a good idea to set a day every week or month, at least, to go out and have a date with your wife, jut the two of you. Don't bring the problems at work and at home along, take that one date to enjoy each other's company and be carefree again, even if it's just for those few hours.

Talk about your day

Yes, one of the tips is as simple as opening up to your wife about your day. You can do it at night, before you both go to bed. Just talk about your day, share your day with her and get closer. Just make a note of having a nice conversation with your life about what's happened in your day.

Play

Don't think that just because you're parents now and are busy adults that you can't play anymore. Physical play is the best way to have an excuse to touch each other and get the romance going. Playing, such as tickling or teasing, helps to lighten the mood and allows you and your wife to have a little fun at home or even in public.

Having romance within the marriage is an important part of making any marriage last and you certainly need it even after you both have babies, even after you celebrate your 25th, 50th, even

75th anniversary. Romance and intimacy are things you have to keep working on so you can get the most out of your marriage. Kids, work, or financial problems should never get in the way of the love you feel for your wife.

Chapter 5 - Fanning the Fires of Passion

"Being deeply loved by someone gives you strength, while loving someone deeply gives you courage."

– Lao Tzu

Sex can be something that's pushed to the sidelines when you've been married for a long time and you have a lot of children and a lot of bills and responsibilities to worry about. Sometimes sex can become just a chore even, and the emotional and intimate side of it is forgotten. Do not forget that sex is an important part of marriage and your compatibility as a couple. It is a great way to get closer to your wife and share deep bonds together. As long as you see sex as a special, intimate, deeply personal experience with your spouse, you're sure to get it right.

In this chapter, you will be given some tips on how to spice up the bedroom and get the passion back in your sheets.

Sex is important

Set a nice romantic mood as background

You can't just demand for sex out of the blue from your wife and expect her to like that. You do have to put on some effort to make her want it too; neither can you expect her to drop her panties because you took her out to dinner. Be subtle and sweet about it and don't get angry or push her if she says she's tired or she's not in the mood. Woo her again, and don't just do it when you're feeling horny, do it every day. Give her a call while you're at work; leave her a bouquet of flowers in a vase in the kitchen with a sweet little note. Small tokens like this will make your wife even more receptive to your sexual advances as well as providing you with some romantic background to get her in the mood.

Unlike a man, a woman's mind is full of connections. A man thinks in a compartmentalized way in which he manages to concentrate on one task at a time, so when he thinks of sex, that's all there is in his mind. For a woman however, having sex is connected to everything else, how you spoke to her in the morning and how you greeted her from work, etc. It is important to keep this in mind so you don't come off as brusque and abrupt when ti comes to sex.

Take your time

As you and your wife get ready to get down and dirty in the bedroom, keep in mind that it take her a little bit longer to get ready for it than you. In fact it can take 20 minutes for her to get ready for sex and eventually reach orgasm. You have to know this and take your time. The key to you getting more sex, if that's what you're looking for, is to help her to enjoy just as much as you do, which is to say, help her reach orgasm too, and taking your time getting her ready is definitely an important part of this.

Experiment

Don't be afraid to move off from your comfort zones and explore new ground. Ask your wife about her favorite fantasies and what excites her and re-enact those fantasies. Find new ways to stimulate arousal, such as visual stimuli (i.e. putting on costumes etc.) or special toys or even experimenting with lubricants, to crank up your sex life. And also, don't be afraid to ask her what she wants. Most women would gladly answer you and even give you some instruction on how to pleasure them.

Have a connection during the act

One thing about women, they seem to enjoy sex more when they feel profoundly connected to the man they are having sex with. A good thing for you to do would be to develop a connection with your lady before you go and do the dirty. Talk to her, complement her, then tell her how beautiful you think she is. Look deep into her eyes and tell her she's the most beautiful woman you've ever laid your eyes on. Sharing a deep connection with your wife as you have sex can increase the pleasure you both feel and get you to a level you haven't been before.

Sex can be something pushed to the sideline when you and your wife get too busy with life. But it is an important part of marriage that you definitely don't want to disregard. Problems in the bedroom can cause deeper problems, such as dissatisfaction in the marriage and even infidelity. It is important that you stay connected romantically and intimately with your wife, no matter how long you've been married.

Chapter 6 - Living your Life and Being a Family Man

"Grow old with me! The best is yet to be."

– Robert Browning

It is important that you manage to balance your life and your goals as well as the time you spend with your family. You need to find that balance or else you could end up losing track of your family or losing track of yourself. Don't think that just because you are married you can no longer pursue your personal goals and the things that bring you fulfillment.

There are many ways that you can allow yourself to be a good father and husband and at the same time strive for your dreams. There are ways that you can provide for your wife's needs without losing track of your own. This chapter will give you some helpful tips on how to manage your time as well as set your boundaries as a man and find fulfillment in your personal life as well as in your married life.

Manage your time off work

A good way of finding more time for yourself outside of work, while, at the same time, giving time to your family is by managing the time you have off of work. By wise and efficient time management, you can get more out of the free time that you have. You can allocate the time you have to spare between your family, your other interests, and self-betterment. By allocating the time that you have to spare between these, you can make sure you are not losing track of one, or spending too much time on another. By managing your time, you can do everything you want to do with the peace of mind that you are still fulfilling your roles as father and husband, as well as your role in the workplace.

Hobbies and Interests

Having hobbies and other interests in your life is a natural inclination and can give you satisfaction and a feeling of accomplishment, even if it's just about the little things. Being busy, men often want to find an escape and clear their head through a certain task or hobby that they have that allows them to relax and focus on just one thing, and the achievement of which then gives them immense satisfaction. Some go into wood working, or building miniatures etc. and these hobbies are things that a man needs to get relaxed.

Just because you have work and a family doesn't mean you have to give these things up, but you will have to schedule it well.

Giving your wife her needs without compromising your own

Sometimes, when you are so bent on satisfying one person, you forget to satisfy someone very important, yourself. It is important that you not lose sight of who you are, your needs, and your own boundaries when it comes to fulfilling the desires of others, particularly your wife. Have a set of boundaries and stand by them, make sure you consider your own comfort and needs when fulfilling the needs of your wife.

Don't lose sight of who you are, even at work

It is important that you have a sense of who you are and your own dignity even when you're at work. Remember your values and principles, remember who you are. What you do does not define your humanity and your being. You have to know what you are willing to do and what you are willing to sacrifice before rushing headlong into any decision.

A good example would be a promotion. Of course you want a promotion, bigger pay and better benefits definitely mean a lot and can change your whole outlook on life, but what does the promotion entail? Do you have to work longer hours? Do you have to travel a lot? Does your base of operations have to move to a different state or city? Does it mean you'll have less time to spend on your family? You have to consider all this and ask yourself, are you really willing to sacrifice the time you can spend with your family for a raise and a promotion? Keep in mind that time is the only thing we can't really earn back once we've spent it and that you can enjoy your children's first steps, their first words, their first day of school only once.

It is also important that you remember that the decision is not just yours to make. The decision you are making will probably affect their whole lives, maybe in a bigger way than it will affect yours, so wouldn't it be a good idea to include them in the decision making process wouldn't it. Surely your wife would appreciate that you asked her, and your children will be thankful for the fact that their opinion was asked. Once you make a decision as a family, you can be sure that they are supporting you, because it was a collective decision, if not, at least you have an idea of how your children feel about the changes and you can help them with the transition better.

Finding the right balance between yourself, your work and your family is important not just for your marriage, but for you as a person. Every human being on earth wants to improve and live a fulfilling life, and you can do this despite the busy work schedule, family activities, and hobbies you may have as long as you manage your time well.

Conclusion

I hope this book has allowed you to understand your wife better and manage your family life well. The thing to do now is to lie your life to the fullest, with your family in hand, and NOT miss out on the fun things you can share with your family.

Here are some helpful websites you can check–out if you believe you need outside help in your marriage:

http://www.marriagebuilders.com/

http://nationalmarriageseminars.com/

http://marriagesupport.meetup.com/

http://www.flrc.org/

Marriage for Women

Your Guide to a Happy, Fulfilling, Intimate Marriage!

Introduction

Congratulations in buying this book!

Having bought this book, it is safe to assume that you are either newly married and are looking for advice, or you are worried about the dying fires of your marriage and need help. You've come to the right place. This book is a short but concise guide in making your marriage work and fostering love in your relationship.

Here you will find tips on how to overcome arguments and how to express yourself in the best way possible, how to keep the intimacy and spice in your relationship, as well as how to juggle the responsibilities of being a mother and wife with your fulfillment as a human being. This book should give you a clear view on what you need to do to make your marriage the happiest it can be.

Chapter 1 – What Makes Marriage Work?

More than 50% of marriages typically end in divorce, and a long lasting marriage is more like a unicorn now, but you have alternatives so that you don't just fall as an extra number on a statistic. If you want to make your marriage work, there are certain things you have to be prepared and be ready for, but you also have to realize what really makes a marriage work.

There are many things that factor in for marriages to work. It all depends on different things, such as your own individual personalities or the dynamics you have in your relationship, but there are certain universal aspects that should always be in a marriage for both parties to stay happy and well-rounded. These are general terms that can mean differently to everyone and can have different manifestations in every relationship, but they always have to be present in any marriage. This chapter will give you simple and quick definitions of these aspects just to give you some idea of what you are striving for in reading this book.

Love

Love is a general term and can mean different things. Often, women find themselves wanting more after a few years of marriage, thinking that the love they have with their husband is no longer enough. Why does this happen?

In the beginning of any relationship, couples often experience a burning, passionate love that can be quite consuming; times like these are often called the spring and summer time of love. This is when you can't get enough of your partner and everything they do and say is just right for you. You are blind to their flaws and everything is perfect, but just like the seasons, these spring and summer times of love don't last. You will start to see the things that you were blind to before and you will become more and more aware of your husband's shortcomings, causing more arguments.

This is often the time when you start to think of 'alternatives' to the situation.

This is normal; this rough patch comes in almost every marriage and you have to try and see that, although it may not be as passionate and consuming as before, the love is still there, only this time you have to foster it. Nurture the love you have for each other until it becomes a nice warm glow of affection and commitment.

Respect

Respect is an important element in marriage. Without respect, you may end up humiliating each other in front of other people, belittling each other, or even betraying each other. Without respect, you cannot have a healthy marriage. If you do not respect and admire the other person, you cannot possibly feel love for him.

You must not lose respect for your husband, not when he says something embarrassing, not when he makes mistakes, not when he makes a bad decision. You have to realize that your role as a wife is to support him, and also to realize that everyone makes mistakes time and again, that's it's normal to do that. You have to respect each other and build each other up, not tear each other down.

Only when you have respect for your husband can you see his struggles with compassion and love. Only with respect can you make your relationship better consciously. If you respect each other's thoughts and emotions, you can both empathize and listen, and through this, you can understand each other better. Having respect for your partner is invaluable if you want to make your marriage last.

Wanting to make it work

Anything worth having will take some degree of effort on your part. NO marriage is perfect. There will always be problems, hardships and difficulties. You will even be at risk of dealing with misunderstandings, especially if you are already together for a long time. There's no way around this, any couple goes through these sorts of problems, but the difference with marriages that last and those that don't is that there are couples who want to work it out, who will work hard to salvage their marriage and see eye to eye on things they disagree on.

You and your husband have to be willing to work hard and give everything you've got for your marriage to work. You have to want to keep it going. This is a conscious choice that can be pivotal in making any marriage last. You can't just let yourself be guided by feelings. Feelings are transient and temporary and you cannot allow your marriage to rely solely on these emotions. You have to make the conscious decision to stay together and work through your differences despite the hardships, and you have to be prepared to put in the effort to fix your problems.

Chapter 2 – Effective Communication in Marriage

Communication is an important part of any relationship and it holds a central part in any marriage. You and your husband have to be able to communicate well in order for you to have a happy marriage. You have to be able to express your feelings within the relationship, and you also have to be a good receiver. You have to be sensitive and really see what your husband means when he says certain things.

Remember that men and women convey their emotions differently. They also have different ways of approaching certain problems. The key is for you to be open and try to interpret what your husband means in the most positive sense.

This chapter delves into the nuances of communication, how to express yourself clearly, and how to listen. Keeping the lines of communication open should be a major part of your agenda to have a happy marriage.

Be open

Starting a conversation with, "You're always at work and never around, you don't even care that I feel all alone do you?" is totally different from saying "I miss you and I wish you were here more often. I feel lonely when I'm alone all the time." These two sentences convey the same essence. The wife feels alone in the marriage because her husband is always too busy with work. She wants her husband to spend more time with her, but starting the conversation with either of these sentences can produce totally different outcomes. As you can see, one of the sentences is extremely negative and can be seen as closed off to explanations.

In the first sentence, you express displeasure over the fact that your husband has no longer time for you, but you are also exaggerating the situation by saying he is NEVER around, words like never and always tend to make the situation seem worse than it is. In the second half of the statement, you are making conclusions of what your husband's intentions are and how he may feel about the situation, making the situation his fault when he probably has no choice and may actually want to spend as much time with you as he can but his work is keeping him from it.

In the second sentence, on the other hand, you are expressing your own feelings in a positive way. You are not making assumptions about your husband; you are simply stating how you feel. You are being open to his input on the situation and on what you can both do to make your situation better. It is important to try opening every conversation in the most diplomatic and positive way possible.

Work around arguments

Arguing over certain points in the marriage is inevitable and will always be present. You just have to know what to do so that whatever you're arguing about doesn't turn into some sort of screaming match where you both say things you'd later regret.

Here are some guidelines in working around arguments:

1. *Don't blow up* - Any argument, no matter how small, tends to get heated if one or both of the parties start getting angry form the get-go. This will never be helpful. You can't allow your feelings to take over. Next time you find yourself disagreeing with your husband, try to approach the problem or disagreement as calmly and objectively as you can. Hear him out and try to understand. When he is done, calmly say your part and ask him to listen to you.

2. *Compromise is key* - After you hear each other out, it is time to find some common ground. Remember that you are not arguing for the sake of knowing who is right, but

for you and your husband to find something to agree on. Standing blindly by what you think is right no matter what will not help either of you. You have to let him influence you and vice versa.

Isn't that what marriage is about, becoming one with the other person? This doesn't mean you have to agree one hundred percent. You just have to understand why your partner thinks in a certain way and go from there. Find common ground and compromise on what you want.

3. *Pick your battles* - Before you get into a heated argument, or even when you're already in one, try to ask yourself if this is worth it? Although there are certain arguments that do have to be sorted out, there are ones that you can consider as rather shallow or superficial, and if you end up fighting all of those out, your marriage can become a rather sour affair. If you end up fighting over everything from which cuts of meat are the best to what kind of cooking oil to use, you can find yourself getting very exhausted very quickly.

   Is it really that important? If you let him make the decision, is it really going to affect your marriage so much? No? Then why argue about it? It may sound cliché, but you have to learn to let certain arguments go.

There is no point in communicating if you are only open to one side of the conversation: yours. You both have to be open to the point of view of each other. Talking loudly over your partner is not helpful and you will never be able to understand each other if you are not open and you don't start the conversation in an open and safe environment. You have to learn to listen to him, too.

Chapter 3 – Sharing the Load

"It is not a lack of love but a lack of friendship that makes unhappy marriages"

- Friedrich Nietzsche

One of the main points of any argument within marriages is the fact that sometimes, either the husband or the wife can feel like they are doing all the work, whether it comes to the finances, the house work or the children. It is important for you to remember that a marriage is about sharing, whether it is wealth, problems, or inner thoughts. You have to be willing to share everything with your husband and you have to be open to share his baggage, too.

One of the things that has to be clarified within the marriage is how you will share these responsibilities, and how you will both be fulfilled, as individuals, within the marriage. In this chapter, you will be given pointers on how to distribute the responsibilities within the marriage, as well as how to be a good wife and mother while also pursuing the dreams you have for your future.

Dividing responsibilities

You and your husband have to develop clear parameters on what you both expect the other to do. You can't just go on assuming that your husband knows what you expect from him and vice versa. You should have an agreement.

If you both have jobs then you really should divide the housework between the two of you. You can start with making a list of the things that have to be done on a day to day basis, and divide them up between you, giving consideration on the time you both have to spare, how convenient it is for you and whether it's of particular interest to you or not, such as one of you may really enjoy cooking, while the other likes to clean. If only one of you is working, then you have to paint a clear picture of what the breadwinner can still do, considering they may be tired all day at work. However, it is still important to keep in mind that housework is also job in itself and can be very tiring.

Help each other out and try to stick to whatever agreements you have. Make sure that you respect each other's responsibilities and give each other space to grow.

Balance your career and being a mother

Motherhood in itself can be considered as a full-time job, and it will take up nearly all of your time as well as your future. Motherhood is a big commitment and it often follows right behind marriage, but being a mother doesn't mean you have to let go of everything you are. There are plenty of ways to balance career and motherhood successfully.

You can be an entrepreneur or a career woman and be a present and caring mother at the same time. Of course, it will not be easy, but you can do it, especially with a supportive husband spurring you on.

1. *Take stock of your Priorities.* It is important that you know what your priorities are and you know what you really want. Is being a career woman that important to you? Is motherhood something you can double task on as a woman? You have to know what your priorities are so that you can go and do what you must without any regrets and second thoughts. Make sure that you are ready to transition. It can be hard for any mother to work while she leaves her children with a babysitter or a day care service. You have to be ready to make these sacrifices in order to achieve what you really want.

2. *Find a way to work and be there for your children at the same time.* Being a mother, you probably can't manage to work eight hours a day in an office or company, and being a working mom used to mean leaving your child all day to earn money, but that is no longer true in the age of the internet. You have so many options that can work for your particular situation. There are many jobs that offer a work

from home option, and you can start your own company right on the internet, making it easy for you to manage it from home. With some proper research, you can definitely find a way to work a schedule around being a mother.

3. *Keep your promises and find the time.* It is important that you are still a dependable mother to your children despite having a career. Try to follow through on your promises. This is a big factor in being a parent. Your children have to know that they can depend on you despite your busy schedule and that you will keep your promises to them when you give it.

   What about when you really have no time to spare? If you find that you really have no time to left, then don't make promises you can't keep. However, make it a point to spend quality time with your children every once in a while.

4. *Include them.* If you can, it would be a good idea to include your family in your side business or career. Find fun things for your children to do so even while you work, you can still spend time with them and have bonding experiences.

Fulfill your husband's needs without losing track of your needs

As a woman, you have to develop clear goals and desires and you have to have a clear picture of what you need from the marriage. Love is a two-way street and in order to be happy, you do not only need to fulfill your husband's needs. You have to feel fulfilled as well. Fulfillment in life, love and intimacy are things that are needed in any relationship. You have to know what you want and also know how to go about getting it.

One of the most important things here is for you to have clear boundaries and limits. You can't lose track of who you are and your personal comfort because you want to make your husband happy, neither can you just compromise your needs for his all the time. It may work for a short time, but having your needs overshadowed by his will sow dissatisfaction in your marriage.

Communicate your needs to him clearly and in a calm and proactive way. His feelings and fulfillment are definitely important, but so are yours. This is where compromise comes in again. You have to find a compromise in both your needs so that you can both be happy with your marriage.

Sharing in marriage does not just mean the bills and the housework. You also have to share life together. This means you have to grow and be better people together. You both have to find fulfillment in both your lives. You both have to be sensitive to each other's needs and goals and incorporate these into your own lives as well as your family's lives so that there will be satisfaction and fulfillment within the marriage.

Chapter 4 – Foster Admiration and Love

Feeling genuine love and admiration for your husband is important, and these are feelings you can foster in yourself. There are many ways for you to focus on the lovable and admirable sides of your husband rather than what causes you dissatisfaction and what you think is lacking. What you choose to focus on is a big factor on how you end up seeing your husband.

How you see people around you depends on your perception and you can change your perception so that you can foster more genuine love in the relationship. This chapter will give you pointers on how you can foster love and affection in your marriage

See your husband in an appreciative light

Focusing on the bad stuff will never get you anywhere. It will only serve to make you feel more dissatisfied with the relationship as well as make your husband feel like he is not good enough. Nagging him on his weaknesses will only cause him to lose his confidence as a man and as your husband. Being negative about things hurts both of you, and it can be even worse if you both have children.

You have to learn to become more appreciative of your husband, and see him in a more positive light. It often happens that you forget the good things when you feel overwhelmed with the bad, and people do tend to remember the negative things more often than the good things, so it will serve you well to remind yourself of the good things more often.

This is an easy exercise you can do to change how you focus on your relationship. Try to think of a happier time. Think about the time when your husband proposed to you. What did you feel back then? Why did you say yes? Or you can think of the day you were married. What did you feel? How did you feel towards your husband?

During these recalling exercises, dig up those feelings of admiration and affection. Remind yourself why you married him and how you felt about him and rekindle those same feelings now.

Be generous with your praise

Praising someone gives them positive feelings and it has even been known that praise within the workplace adds to employee productivity. Praise is not hard to give out. It is pretty easy and it costs you nothing. Praising your husband when does something good or praising his good qualities can be more effective than berating him for not doing something. Make giving praise a regular activity you can do to build up your husband's self-esteem as well as strengthen the bonds of your relationship.

Try to think of your husband's good traits and mention at least one every day. You can do it spontaneously. For example, you can say, "I love how you take care of us," over dinner, or as he leaves for work, or whenever you think is best. This way, you are reinforcing the good things about him that you love, and you are filling your mind with the positive rather than the negative aspects, which means you are inclining your mind to note the good things rather than the bad. This way, you will be more capable of finding good things to cherish about your relationship.

Maintain realistic expectations of your husband

It is normal and understandable to have expectations of one's husband. The problem only arises if those expectations are unreasonable and unrealistic. You have to make sure that your expectations are things that your husband can easily fulfill. Don't you think it is unfair to demand things that are just impossible for your spouse to fulfill? Not only is it unfair, it can also be hurtful and it only adds stress and dissatisfaction in the relationship.

Before you make any requests or expect anything, do a reality check. See if your expectations are doable for your husband. Whenever you have unrealistic expectations, it was as if you were laying down a trap for your husband, expecting something that is quite obvious he will not be able to fulfill. A good thing to do will be to talk to each other about your expectations, not just your expectations of him but what he expects of you as well.

List down your expectations and do a back and forth, what is realistic and doable, and what is unrealistic and impossible. This way, you have clear and realistic views on each other's abilities and expectations.

Love and admiration are emotions that we generally think we have no control over, but the truth is we can teach ourselves to be more appreciative and generous, through which we can foster feelings of love and admiration. Sometimes, such feelings are just lost to us, buried under mounds of negativity and dissatisfaction, but this does not mean that we can't dig up these feelings again and cherish them.

Chapter 5 – Keeping the Fires of Passion Burning

"I have, for the first time, found what I can truly love, I have found you."

-   *Charlotte Bronte*

It is often a running joke in TV and movies that once a couple gets married, the sexual excitement ends, and you can say it is true for some, or even many, of married couples. When the children come, it becomes even harder to give time for each other and just have fun. Intimacy and sex can sometimes get lost amidst the daily grind. Sometimes, you both come to bed and you are both just so tired that you fall asleep straight away, not even having a conversation at least. And then, before you know it, months have passed this way.

You just end up going through the motions. You realize that you have lost the spark of passion, but don't worry, this does not mean it's too late. There is still a chance for you and your husband to rekindle the fires of passion in your marriage, or if you're newlywed, to keep the fires burning. This chapter will give you some insight on how to keep the intimacy and have a healthy and satisfying sex life after marriage.

The importance of sex in marriage

Sex is a fun, special and intimate act that you do with your partner. It can make you closer to each other, not to mention satisfying your very normal lady urges. Having less sex after marriage can take its toll after a while.

Although relationships should not be based on sexual chemistry alone, making love with your husband is an important part of marriage and commitment and it's something you mustn't forget.

Try to be receptive with your husband when he tries to initiate sex and don't think that because you're a woman you can't do the initiating. You can try different, new and fun ways to get in the mood, from using toys, to watching 'shows' that can help you to spice up your sexual life.

Have fun and be open to trying new things with your husband without violating any personal boundaries you may have. Have fun with each other and make it exciting. You can do this with simple things like playing around or tickling each other, finding any excuse to touch each other, and slowly transition into sex.

The importance of intimacy

Intimacy here doesn't just pertain to sex in this context. Intimacy means being close to your husband and being able to share your deepest thoughts and secrets with him without any fear of being judged. This means allowing yourself to become intimate and vulnerable with your husband. This is an important aspect of your marriage.

This does not mean that you are showing your weakness. This just means that you have the courage to be yourself and show your silliest, sweetest, most shameful sides to him. Being willing to do it because you want to get closer and because you are not afraid of getting hurt means that you trust him enough not to hurt you or belittle your emotions about things. This also means being honest about how you feel and what you want, as well as your secrets and desires. Having no secrets within the relationship is important for you both to reach a level of intimacy that will help to make your relationship last.

Have regular and spontaneous dates

Sometimes, you and your husband can end up super busy, so busy that you no longer have time for each other, but the truth is, you can always make time and find a way around your busy schedule to be together, just the two of you. A date doesn't mean you have to go out to some expensive restaurant or watch a big expensive show. This is hardly possible, especially if you already have children. You can opt for something simple, such as making a nice dinner and putting the kids to bed early and watching an old movie you both love, or going out to the patio and watching the stars together. You can do this easily, and an hour and a half of bonding is better than nothing at all.

You can have a schedule of when you should date once a week and make sure to keep the date. Choose a day that works for the both of you and make sure to have all the sides covered. Get a babysitter beforehand and make sure all the chores that need to be done are finished. Added to this, you can also have spontaneous dates, going out for a quick drink will do or even just having dinner out on the porch. If you set your mind to it, you are sure to find ways to be together and be intimate.

Chapter 6 – Making it Last

Your marriage is a sanctified union between you and your husband. You both swore to love and cherish each other as long as you both live and you can make it work and make it last. This chapter delves into the main points of living a long and happy married life.

The importance of compromise and consideration

You cannot expect to be in a healthy relationship without compromising and being considerate. You have to understand your partner and how he feels about things, and you have to be willing to give in too; in fact, you both have to. You have to find the balance between compromise and standing by your ideals.

Think of how your husband feels and be empathetic to how he feels. Be willing to give him the upper hand from time to time.

The importance of shared experiences

It is important that you and your husband not only reside in the same home together, but that you LIVE together. This means that you enjoy life together, share your interests with each other, or find new interests together. You are never too old to have adventures together

Marriage is a commitment you make to yourself and another person, promising to stay together, to love and cherish each other through the years, despite the hardships and struggles. You cannot do this if you have lost love and respect for that person, but it is important to note that love and respect are decisions you make. You can CHOOSE to love and respect a person consciously, and you can CHOOSE to make your marriage work with this person. You can put in the effort to have a healthy and happy marriage. You can make your marriage last.

Websites you can check out for counseling and seminars to help with your marriage:

http://www.marriagebuilders.com/

http://nationalmarriageseminars.com/

http://marriagesupport.meetup.com/

http://www.flrc.org/

Conclusion

I hope this book was able to give you some useful tips in having a happy, healthy, fulfilling and long lasting marriage. You just have to follow the tips given above to really get to know your husband and have true intimacy between you so you can have a positive and happy married life.

Get out there and share the love to your family and your husband. You can be a great wife and mother, as well as your own independent woman!

Finally, if you enjoyed this book, please take time to post a review on Amazon. It'll be greatly appreciated.

Thank you and good luck!

Marriage and Sex:

Why sex matters to keep romance alive!

Introduction

I want to thank you and congratulate you for downloading the book, *"**Marriage and Sex: Why sex matters to keep romance alive!**"*

This book contains proven steps and strategies on how to achieve a successful marriage by increasing the quality of your sex life.

The longer you've been married to each other, the more roles you end up taking. With each day, you become more of a mother, father, provider, or homemaker and less of a lover. Some couples feel that as long as they are able to fulfill these other roles, it should be enough to keep their home and marriage intact. Yet, studies reveal that it doesn't make much difference how many kids you've got, how long you've been together, or whether you live in a low-income or a high-income household. The fact is: Lack of sex and intimacy result to unhappy marriages and broken homes.

Sex between married couples is different from sex between non-married couples. Instead of a quick, physical interaction, sex in marriage becomes a deep, meaningful, affirming connection which strengthens the couple's relationship. Sleeping with the same person for years mean that you know exactly where and how he/she wants to be touched. You know what each gesture, each sigh, and each look means. Furthermore, the longer you've lived together under the same roof, the more comfortable you've grown with each other. Sex between married couples is free from inhibitions. Instead, the act itself becomes an expression of total acceptance. Because of this, sex becomes more pleasurable and more satisfying. So why aren't you doing it as often as you should?

A lot of stuff tends to get lost in a typical household: socks, spontaneity, sex...

Through this book, you will learn:

- the importance of sex in marriage
- sex positions that your husband/wife will love
- why couples lose their sex drive and strategies on how to regain it
- secrets for maintaining a great sex life

Thanks again for downloading this book, I hope you enjoy it!

the trademark owner. All trademarks and brands within this book are for clarifying purposes only and are the owned by the owners themselves, not affiliated with this document.

Chapter 1

Why is Sex Important in Marriage?

➤ Sex is unique between you and your spouse.

Among the many ideal characteristics of marriage is that it enables couples to share sexual intimacy with each other and *only* with each other. The fact that the two of you are married makes sex more valuable because it becomes a pleasurable experience that you can uniquely and exclusively share with your spouse and not with anyone else. Without sex, your husband/wife is literally reduced to the role of a roommate. Thus, the fact that sex is essential to a successful marriage is certainly an understatement.

➤ Sex makes married life a whole lot easier.

When married couples allow sex life to jump out of the window, this creates a massive strain in the relationship. This may not always be obvious but little by little, the effects manifest themselves through lack of patience, irritability, insecurities, doubt, and subconscious resentment. On the other hand, married couples who have active sex lives tend to be more relaxed. They become happier, more tolerant, and more open-minded. Simply put, sex in marriage helps in smoothing over the trials that married couples inevitably encounter on a daily basis. You'll be surprised to find out how, after solving the sexual issues in your marriage, everything else will eventually fall into place.

➤ Sex is a form of intimate communication.

Sex in marriage involves a deeper level of communication which you can't have with just anyone. Having sex and talking about sex with your spouse makes you vulnerable to him/her and this is a beautiful thing. This validates emotions of trust, honesty, and acceptance. Telling your spouse where and how you would like to be touched brings you to a comfort level which you will never feel with anyone else. Your husband/wife is that one person in the universe who can see, understand, and appreciate you like no other. With that knowledge in mind, each time you have sex, it becomes more than just a physical act but a powerful emotional experience of giving and receiving with no fear of rejection or judgment.

There is a unique energy between husbands and wives that cannot be expressed in any other way than through sex. But the less couples have sex, the less they become in tune with each other. Eventually, both end up feeling as if the other is a stranger. Come to think of it, having a stranger in your bed is unsettling and frightening. When this happens, all those feelings of trust, safety, and security which are all vital ingredients in marriage just vanish.

> ➤ **Sex affirms your spouse's value.**

The typical situation in problematic marriages goes like this:

The husband wants to have more sex while the wife doesn't. For the husband, sex is what enables him to feel close to his wife. The wife cannot understand why he needs sex in order to feel close. She doesn't see why he can't achieve a sense of closeness through talking, cuddling, and just spending time with her. Meanwhile, the husband cannot understand why sexual intercourse does not make his wife feel close to him. Then, the wife begins wondering why sex is so important to her husband. She begins wondering whether there's something wrong with her.

The reason for this is because men and women are wired differently. While women associate romance with emotions, men's perception of romance is strongly associated with sexual affirmation. For men, sex is a verification of their vitality. Sex, especially certain forms of sex such as oral sex, affirm his manhood and makes him feel that you love, respect, and honor all of him.

Here's another typical real life scenario:

The wife worries why her husband lacks interest in her. She does her best to be attractive from spending long hours at the gym to walking around the house in lingerie that are too slutty for her tastes. Yet, the most response she gets from him is a reminder to iron his shirt in the morning. She begins to worry why her husband no longer finds her sexy. This realization damages her self-esteem. She starts feeling embarrassed for having to constantly seduce him. She begins to worry that he's seeing someone else or that she's just not as hot as younger women. Soon, she develops resentment towards her husband.

In both cases, the ultimate effect is emotional detachment between the couples.

What men fail to understand is that their sexual advances make their wives feel special. She needs constant reassurance that you love her and that you still find her attractive after all these years. In other words, your sexual advances affirm her value. All in all, whether you're a man or a woman, you like to feel wanted and needed in your marriage.

> ➢ **Sex protects your marriage.**

Lack of sex in marriage brings about infidelity which often leads to divorce. Sexual desires are meant to be shared and not repressed. All of us possess an inborn desire to have sex. But when couples are no longer able to obtain romance, intimacy, and pleasure in their marriage, it creates a void within them which makes them vulnerable to sexual temptation. They end up seeking this much-needed sense of joy and satisfaction elsewhere. It may be through extramarital affairs, sexual fantasies about other men/women, masturbation and pornography, etc.

> ➢ **Sex helps you keep in touch with who you are as a couple and as an individual.**

If you've been married for several years, this means you've inevitably acquired new roles other than that of a lover. You become a parent, a provider, head of the household, etc. You become too absorbed with being mom or dad that little by little, you forget who you were as a couple. Worse, you forget who you are as an individual. Dinner dates are replaced by family dinners. Sexy time is replaced by playtime with kids. Personal hobbies that you used to be passionate about are replaced by PTA meetings, soccer games, and ballet recitals. Add to that the hours required for housework and the demands of your career and you'll certainly be left with zero time for your spouse, let alone yourself. There are some couples who think this is okay. After all, you're expected to make certain sacrifices for your children. However, once the children are all grown up and have left the house, most couples are surprised to realize that they have nothing in common with each other anymore.

This is why increasing the frequency and the quality of sex in your marriage is so important. Sex with your spouse reminds you what brought you together in the first place. This doesn't just pertain to the physical attraction but also to the emotional and mental connection that made you want to spend the rest of your life with that person. Sex with your husband/wife will remind you that you're more than just a mom/dad but vital sexual beings with needs and desires.

> **Sex allows you to stay together longer.**

Physical illness can cause a great strain in your married life. That said, sex is one way in which you can be healthy together. Scientific studies show that sex has several positive effects to your overall wellness. Sexual intercourse stimulates your immune system and improves your stress levels. Older married men who have sex regularly are less prone to developing prostate cancer. Likewise, sex regulates hormone levels so women who have sex more frequently suffer less from menopausal symptoms. Sex also lessens the risk for heart disease in both men and women.

Chapter 2

Best Sex Positions for Him

> ➢ **Doggie Style**

Why your husband will love it:

Generally, men love rear-entry positions because they place them in a position of control. This means that he can regulate the thrusts, to slow it down or speed it up depending on what works best for him. The doggie style is a very primal position and such positions make him feel very manly.

Furthermore, this sex position allows deep penetration so this makes him feel like he's giving you all that he's got and likewise, he's taking all that you have. Additionally, your husband gets a great view of your rear.

Why you'll love it too:

This position can provide you with a full sensation that's really intense.

How to do it right:

- First, you'll need to get down on your hands and on your knees.

- Make sure that your legs are spread slightly apart.

- Your husband will then get down on his knees and then enter you from the rear. He may either place his hands on your back or he may grab your waist if he wants to perform harder thrusts. Alternatively, he may hold on to your shoulders. Or if you're in the mood for rough sex, allow him to grab your hair.

- If you want your husband to go deeper into you, meet his thrusts by pushing your backside against him.

- If you want to change angles, you may lower your body onto the ground.

- You may also make use of your free hand to stimulate your clitoris. Or you may take your husband's hand and guide it towards your love button.

- Maintaining this position can be a bit problematic on your part unless you've got great arm strength. Here's a valuable tip: Try performing this position on the floor by the bed. This way, you can remove your weight off your hands and rest the upper part of your body.

> **Cowgirl Position**

Why your husband will love it:

Most husbands wish their wives would do Woman on Top positions more often. Nobody wants a passive partner in bed. But more than that, one of your husband's primary goals during sex is to please you. Knowing that he is able to satisfy you physically boosts his ego. Additionally, the cowgirl position provides him with a full view of your body. Remember, men are very visual creatures.

Why you'll love it too:

This position can provide you with a sense of empowerment. Being on top will allow you to regulate the pace, depending on what you think works best for you. More importantly, this ensures that his penis hits all your right spots. Thus, your chances of achieving orgasm in this position ranges from huge to inevitable.

Furthermore, if you'd like to tease your husband or prolong his pleasure, this power position can help you do that.

How to do it right:

- Your husband should be lying on his back.

- Afterwards, you'll have to straddle him while you are kneeling. Make sure that your legs are situated on either side of your husband's waist.

- Move yourself up and down. If you want to adjust the angle, do this by simply leaning forward or backward. Doing so will provide more stimulation for your clitoris and your outer vagina.

- You may choose to rest your hands on your hubby's chest. To maintain intimacy during sex, it's best to remain in contact with whatever body part you can get hold of. That's the other advantage of this position. It allows eye contact between you and your partner so lovemaking becomes more intimate.

- Try having sex in this position with the lights on. This way, he can see your curves. Let go of your feelings of self-consciousness. Also, since your husband gets a full view of your face, drive him mad by biting your lip or with sexy facial expressions. You're in the spotlight so put on a show!

> **Reverse Cowgirl Position**

Why your husband will love it:

He'll love it for the simple reason that it gives him an awesome view of your butt.

Why you'll love it too:

You'll love this for the same reasons that you'll love the cowgirl position. The difference is that this'll keep your frontal curves hidden from your hubby's view. This one's a recommended baby step if you're not ready to get past your feelings of self-consciousness.

How to do it right:

- First, ask your hubby to lie on his back.

- Then, assume a kneeling position and with your back to him, straddle your husband. Your knees must be on either side of his body.

- Perform the trusts by moving up and down, slow or fast or alternate.

- If you want to adjust the angle, just lean backward or forward.

- If you want to switch things up a bit, try making slow grinding maneuvers with your hips.

➢ **Bodyguard Position**

Why your husband will love it:

This is basically just a classic standing position. Men tend to love it because it's perfect for let's-have-sex-here-and-now moments. This is something that you can do when you're standing by the sink in the kitchen or in cramped rooms when you sneak off for an afternooner. Furthermore, by holding on to your waist, he'll be able to perform harder, deeper thrusts. With this position, the mood can easily change from romantic to rough.

Why you'll love it too:

Even though it's a position for quickies, the Bodyguard isn't necessarily devoid of intimacy. With your back pressed against his front, your husband can nibble on your ear, kiss your neck, or whisper sweet, sexy words while having sex.

How to do it right:

- Begin with the both of you standing upright. You should both be facing the same direction.

- Then, allow your hubby to enter you from behind.

- Meet his thrusts by pushing your body back onto his.

> ## Bendover Position

Why your husband will love it:

This is another rear-entry standing position that's perfect for quickies. Much like the doggie style, this is another primal position that will allow him to reach in front and grab any part of your body that he pleases. Or if you'll allow it, he can grab your hair and bring out his inner caveman.

Why you'll love it too:

The Bendover is a great deal less intimate than the Bodyguard position. That said, it's not such a bad idea to bring out your wild side from time to time. While making love, you can guide his hands to your front so he can fondle your breasts or play with your clitoris.

How to do it right:

- Basically, all you need to do is to assume the Bodyguard position first.

- Then, once he's in, simply lean over while stretching your arms out. Do this until your hands are able to come in contact with the floor.

- While your hubby is thrusting in and out of you, you may choose to meet his trusts by pushing back up against him or to just let him take control.

- Balance yourself with your arms and with your hands close to your feet.

Chapter 3

Best Sex Positions for Her

> ➤ **Spooning Position**

Why your wife will love it:

For most women, sex is all about the romance and the intimacy. The spooning position provides your wife with a feeling of safety. This position also creates a snug fit in a woman's vagina so she'll feel that you're bigger. Your wifey will get more stimulation in the vaginal wall. It's also a great position for slow sex during lazy afternoons.

Why you'll love it too:

Apart from the tighter fit, this is the perfect remedy for morning wood! Wake up in the morning, roll over towards your wife's side of the bed, and make a connection. Sure, this position is not meant for deep penetration but it will allow you to reach into the front and stroke her bits. You can also whisper naughty words to your mate.

How to do it right:

- While facing the same way, both you and your wife should lie on your sides.

- Position yourself behind her and enter her gently from behind. You're wife's gonna have to bring her top leg slightly forward to ease your entry. Likewise, you'll need to lean over a little.

- Wrap your arms around your wife for added intimacy.

- If you want to add more power to your thrusts, grab the top side of your wife's waist.

> **Butterfly Position**

Why your wife will love it:

With this position, your penis will come directly in contact with her upper vaginal walls. This means your wife will get major G-spot stimulation leading to multiple orgasms. More than that, this position promotes intimacy through eye contact. It's also a good position for verbal and non-verbal communication during intercourse.

Why you'll love it too:

Apart from the fact that you'll be giving your wifey multiple O's, this modified missionary position places you in a power position, allowing you to control the pace of lovemaking.

How to do it right:

- Ask your wife to lie on her back. Her hips should be positioned close to the edge of your bed.

- Assume a standing position at the foot of the bed. Then, lift her hips upwards.

- Allow your wife to rest her thighs on your chest. Meanwhile, lay her calves on either side of your shoulders. Alternatively, you can have her legs wrapped around your waist.

- If you want to make your thrusts more vigorous, grab her thighs.

➢ **Criss Cross Position**

Why your wife will love it:

The Criss Cross provides women with maximum clitoral stimulation.

Why you'll love it too:

This position creates a tighter feel. Even when you're not on top, it's still a dominant position where you're able to control the thrusts. More than that, it allows deeper, more powerful strokes.

How to do it right:

- This position can be done on the bed or a on a table.

- Have your wife lie down on her back. Then, lift her legs so that they are pointing skyward.

- Then, stand up straight and penetrate her. While doing so, your wife should make sure that her legs are straight.

- Help your wife cross her legs at her ankles. After doing this, you'll immediately feel the tighter fit. The more she crosses her legs, the tighter her vagina will feel.

- Alternate your thrusts from deep and hard to quick and shallow.

➢ **Lotus Position**

Why your wife will love it:

The Lotus is the most intimate sexual position ever invented, dating back from ancient times. In tantra, this is known as a sacred sex position that enables man and wife to connect not just physically but also emotionally and spiritually while having intercourse. This position requires you to look at each other face to face so you can maintain eye contact during sex or engage in deep and passionate kisses.

Why you'll love it too:

Apart from the fact that you'll feel closer to your significant other, this provides your wife easy access to your back. She can provide you with an erotic back rub while making love to you. This is also a good position if you enjoy having your ears and your neck licked.

How to do it right:

- Assume a cross-legged sitting position on bed. You may also choose to do this on the floor or on any flat surface. Just imagine that you're about to do yoga.

- Then, ask your wife to lower herself onto you while facing you.

- Her arms and her legs should end up wrapped around your body.

- Do the same thing and envelop her in your arms.

- Your wife will then make back and forth rocking movements.

- As she does this, kiss your wife's neck and gaze into her face. Whisper some loving words to her. You can tell her how lovely she looks or how good it feels making love to her.

> **Pearly Gates Position**

Why your wife will love it:

This is a position that will make your wife feel exposed. Nevertheless, she'll love it. She'll like the sense of abandon that this position will provide her with. Because it's somewhat similar to the spooning position, she'll also feel a sense of security and intimacy.

Why you'll love it too:

This is a simple yet inventive position that's rarely done by couples in bed. Furthermore, it'll give you easy access to her front side if you want to masturbate her while entering her from behind.

How to do it right:

- The two of you should lie on the bed while facing the same way.

- Make sure that your knees are bent and that your feet are flat on the bed.

- Ask your wife to lie on her back on top of you. It's just like spooning but the difference is you're both looking upward.

- Assist your wife in balancing herself. Put your arms around her waist or her chest. Ask her to spread out her arms and her legs.

- Then, keeping your feet flat on the bed, thrust into her. You can also reach in front of your wife to give her a hand, so to speak.

- Make this lovemaking position more intimate by kissing her neck and uttering words of affection into your wife's ear.

Chapter 4

Why Couples Lose their Sex Drive and How to Fix It

There used to be a time when you can't seem to get your hands off each other. But now, whenever one of you wants to have sex, the other's almost always not up for it. Perhaps you still love each other. That much hasn't changed. So what happened? Is it possible to get all "sexed out"?

Before you allow feelings or resentment or guilt to creep into your marriage, you need to understand that there are many factors that affect your libido. These influences range from the kind of job that you have to the stuff that you pop into your mouth. The good news is these factors are modifiable.

➢ Physical Exhaustion

Most couples wake up early in the morning, go to work, come home, fix dinner, and by the time they hit the sack, they're just plumb tired, not just physically but mentally as well.

The solution? If you want to achieve more O's then you'd better get more Z's first. Lack of sleep diminishes your libido. Try having sex in the morning. Wake up, gargle, and then get it on. You'll observe that sexy time after a good night's rest is so much better than forcing yourselves to do it before bedtime.

➢ Your Hormones are Messed Up

If you're suffering from hormonal imbalances, then it's no wonder your libido has gone loco. Once a woman hits her 40's , she'll experience a decrease in her estrogen levels. This can subsequently lower her libido. More than that, low estrogen levels cause her vagina to dry up, making intercourse painful.

It's not just menopausal women who experience this problem. Individuals with underactive thyroid may possess low sex drives as well. Furthermore, women who use certain types of hormonal contraceptives claim to experience loss of libido.

The solution? Lube up! There are endless variations of lubricants to suit the needs and preferences of different couples. You may also talk to your doctor about hormone replacement therapy to determine whether it's for you. If you suspect that hormonal contraceptives are the cause of your waning sex drive, then you'll need to discuss it with your GP and look for possible family planning alternatives.

> ## You're Not Drinking Enough Water

Dehydration can kill your libido not to mention cause downstairs dryness in women. Men, on the other hand, end up having low sperm counts.

The solution? Rehydrate.

> ## You're Drinking Too Much Alcohol

While a little bit of alcohol can put you in the mood, it can prevent women from achieving orgasm. Likewise, it causes several sexual difficulties in men ranging from erectile dysfunction to ejaculatory problems. Additionally, excessive alcohol consumption causes dehydration.

The solution? Limit alcoholic drinks to two glasses before having sex. (Or less if you have poor alcohol tolerance)

> ➤ **You Sleep With Your Phone**

Ideally, the bedroom should be a gadget-free zone. Unless we're talking sex toys. It's easy to get sucked into the world of social media or sports or show business if you bring your laptop to bed. The same can be said about T.V. shows. Keep on with this habit and it'll become more and more difficult for you to think about, much less initiate, sexual intercourse.

The solution? Turn your bedroom into your very own sensual shrine. The bedroom should only be used for two reasons: snoozing and sexing. Thus, bringing work to bed is a big no-no. More than that, remove everything that will remind you of work or chores. Paperwork, shopping lists, and bills don't belong in the bedroom.

Keep in mind that great sex involves all the senses. Use dim lighting. Play relaxing music. Increase your libido by lighting scented candles or incense. Scents that can arouse your wife include vanilla, patchouli, and musk. Scents that can arouse your husband include pumpkin spice, lavender, and citrus.

> ➤ **Your Meds Are Ruining Your Sexual Appetite**

As people age, the prescriptions just seem to pile up. Certain anti-depressants, drugs for heartburn, and medication for hypertension can decrease your sex drive.

The solution? Check with your doctor if any of your prescribed meds have libido-lowering side effects. If yes, talk about alternatives.

> ### ➢ It's Just the Same Ol' Same Ol'

Getting into a sex rut is a number one libido killer. It's inevitable for couples who have been together for so long to form a routine that they're comfortable with. But when things get too predictable, there's just nothing more to look forward to. You've already stripped away the mystery and the only way to make up for it is through variety. Switch things up before your partner starts looking for excitement elsewhere.

The solution? Communication. Sit with your spouse and talk about your deepest (even your darkest) desires. Listen to each other in a non-judgmental way. Compromise. Let each other know what you're willing to try. If your partner's fantasies turn out to be a little too much for you, rather than saying "No.", simply say "Not yet." Because hey, you'll never know... Give and take. Make sure that you exercise fairness on considering each other's carnal wishes.

> ### ➢ You Wouldn't Even Dare Sleep With Yourself

Have you looked at yourself in the mirror lately? How well have you been taking care of yourself? When people age, they gain weight, their skin loses its elasticity, and other undesirable changes occur. The less attractive you feel, the lower your libido becomes. This decreases your confidence in the bedroom, causing you to shy away from intimacy.

The solution? Take care of yourself. More than just maintaining proper hygiene, prep your body for sex by shaving your legs/nether regions or wearing underwear that makes you feel sexy. More importantly, boost each other's confidence. Give each other sincere compliments. Don't be afraid to tell your partner what you love most about him/her. Kiss that body part frequently. If your partner has made an effort to look more appealing in bed (even if it's as simple as spraying on some perfume), make sure that you let him/her know that you've noticed and appreciate it. Make an effort to look good and do it together. Help each other to age gracefully. Exercise together. Eat healthy together. Bathe each other.

Chapter 5

How to Maintain a Great Sex Life: More Tips from Real Happy Couples

➤ **Make a sex jar.**

If you can make a Christmas list, then you sure as hell can make a bucket list for sex. Write down all of your hottest fantasies on small pieces of paper and throw them in your sex jar. You can fill the jar with anything from new sexual positions that you'd like to try to exotic places that you'd like to have sex in. Each time you're feeling adventurous, pick a paper from the jar and just do what it says. If you can't do it then and there, set a date.

➤ **Incorporate food with sex.**

Before making love, feed each other aphrodisiacs like strawberries or oysters. Pour chocolate syrup or ice cream into each other's bodies and lick it off. Better yet, turn your body into an aphrodisiac buffet by adorning yourself with grapes, cucumber slices, etc. and invite your spouse to feast on you.

➤ **Formulate your own codes for sex.**

Make a gesture or a word for sex that only the both of you will understand. Tease each other in public. Foreplay doesn't necessarily have to happen immediately prior to sex. It can start as early as before he/she leaves for work in the morning. You can leave a sexy note in his/her briefcase/purse or even leave handcuffs in his/her car. Communicate through subtle signs and sexy glances over dinner to increase each other's anticipation for "dessert"!

> **Try no-orgasm sex.**

Yes, you read it right. Couples make the mistake of treating orgasm as the end-all and be-all of sexual intercourse. From time to time, try to just connect with each other… feeling each other, being one with each other, and taking your time. This may take some getting used to but once you get the hang of it, you'll realize how it can actually strengthen your bond and deepen your intimacy.

> **Alter your evening routine.**

When you follow a certain routine every evening, it's easy to just get comfortable and fall asleep. Shaking up your repertoire (ex. feeding each other dessert, playing a game, etc.) can open up other possibilities apart from sleep.

> **Get naked more often.**

This opens up the possibility for more frequent sex. Sleeping in the nude can actually bring about sexier wet dreams that will help get you in the mood.

> **Have sex one day before her period arrives.**

Sounds weird? The accumulation of blood causes her uterus to be heavy. Because of this, contractions become more intense during orgasm. More than that, during this time, her clitoris and her labia become more sensitive.

> ➤ **Play with each other.**

Rigorous activity before sex releases feel good chemicals in your body. So go out on a run, take a few laps, chase each other around the bedroom, or just tickle each other in bed.

> ➤ **Masturbate with each other.**

Or engage in non-intercourse sex. Apart from the fact that you will be providing each other with a visual delight, it'll be like taking each other back to the good ol' days when you were young and not quite ready to have sex yet. Talk about a sexy blast from the past!

> ➤ **Explore each other's erogenous zones.**

Don't just limit yourself to pleasuring your partner's genitalia. Caress, kiss, and lick each other's hot spots such as the nape of the neck, the ears, the back, and the inner thighs. Men should pay more attention to their wives' sacrum. Likewise, women should explore their husbands' perineum.

> ➤ **Experiment with tantric sex.**

If it worked for the royals of ancient times, then it might be worth checking out, right? Learn some new moves from the wisdom of the past. Tantric sex is all about prolonging each other's pleasure to give each other powerful orgasms. But more than that, it's also about deepening your connection in the physical, emotional, mental, and spiritual level. That's the way sex in marriage is supposed to be.

Conclusion

Thank you again for downloading this book!

I hope this book was able to help you to understand and appreciate the importance of sex in improving your marriage.

Marriage is such a special and sacred bond. Don't allow that bond to be fractured by lack of physical intimacy.

The next step is to follow these tips and strategies to rekindle that waning flame. Remember that this is more than just bringing lust back into the sheets. Instead, it's about communicating and affirming each other's value in the relationship.

Finally, if you enjoyed this book, then I'd like to ask you for a favor, would you be kind enough to leave a review for this book on Amazon? It'd be greatly appreciated!

Thank you and good luck!

Sex Positions:

Your Guide to the 50 Best Sex Positions for a sexy marriage!

Check Out My Other Books!

Thanks for downloading my book! I am a firm believer that in order to have a fulfilling family life-one must be properly prepared and understand the fundamentals of relationships, how to be a good parent, and live an exciting and adventurous sex life. As you can see, I have written a series of multiple books on marriage, sex, and parenting. If you are looking to learn more about how to improve your marriage, sex and dating life, family life, etc.-please check out my other books! Simply click on the links below or search the titles below to check them out.

Parenting:

Parenting 101: 20 strategies to follow to raise well-behaved children

Raising Your Kids: Time Management for Parents for Stress-Free Parenting

Sex (General):

Sex Positions: Your Guide to the 50 Best Sex Positions for a sexy marriage!

Tantra Sex: The Beginner's Guide to 25 Tantra Techniques

Tantric Massage: Your Guide to the Best 30 Tantric Massage Techniques

BDSM Positions: The Beginner's Guide to 30 BDSM Techniques

Sex: Spice Up Your Sex Life! How to be maintain an awesome sex life with your partner and live your wildest sexual fantasies!

Sex Games: 35 Naughty Sex Games to make your Sex Life Hot!

Sex For Women:

Sexting: Sexting Tips for Women: 100 tips to turn him on!

Sex Positions for Women: The Ultimate Guide to the 50 Best Techniques to Turn Your Man On!

Talk Dirty: How to talk to get your man aroused and in the mood for sex!

Sex: The Hottest Tips for Better Orgasms!

Sex for Men:

Sex Positions for Men: The Ultimate Guide to the 50 Best Techniques to Turn Her On!

Dirty Talk: Talking Dirty for Men: 200 Examples to Get Your Girl Aroused and in the Mood for Sex!

Sex: Make her beg for more and be the best she's ever been with in bed!

Marriage:

Dating:

Contents

Sex and Successful Relationships

How to be Sexy in the Bedroom and How to Maintain a Great Sex Life

50 Best Sex Positions for Men and Women

Introduction

I want to thank you and congratulate you for downloading the book, *"Sex Positions: Your Guide to the 50 Best Sex Positions for a sexy marriage!"*

This book contains proven steps and strategies on how to develop a more meaningful, satisfying, and lasting relationship with your spouse through sex.

Every couple goes through a honeymoon period where they just can't seem to take their hands off each other. But as other aspects of the relationship grow more important, couples begin to realize changes in their sexual appetites. When one of you suddenly wants to make love less than the other, this leads to bitterness and disillusionment.

A waning libido is a common problem among couples who have been sleeping with each other for years and years. Contrary to what most might think, it's not just because you no longer find your partner attractive. Often, it's because *you* no longer find *yourself* attractive. When you look into the mirror, cringe, and decide that even *you* wouldn't sleep with you, this destroys your self-esteem. And in order to feel aroused, you need to feel that you are desired and that you're worthy of being wanted. Through this book, you'll find tips on how to be sexy in the bedroom. You'll learn that feeling sexy and having great sex is not about defying the sands of time. It's about getting the years to work *for* you instead of *against* you.

Sex and stagnancy don't mix. Couples who make a continuous effort to re-explore each other's bodies and find new ways to please each other are bound to last longer than those who don't. In this book, you'll find 50 of the best sex positions ranging from positions that can give her multiple orgasms to positions that can make him feel like the ultimate alpha male between the sheets.

Thanks again for downloading this book, I hope you enjoy it!

Chapter 1

Sex and Successful Relationships

➤ **Sex connects you.**

And not just physically but mentally and emotionally as well. Most couples will agree that nothing can make you feel closer to your partner than when you're making love with him/her. The mere act of being naked together makes you vulnerable to each other. Thus, the act of lovemaking fosters feelings of trust and acceptance. When sex is a satisfactory experience, you both feel a sense of security in each other's arms. After sex, the feel-good hormone oxytocin is released into your bloodstream. This provides you both with a sense of calm and contentment, therefore enabling you to bond with each other.

➤ **Sex makes your relationship smoother.**

When couples who have been together for a long time start to neglect each other in the bedroom, this creates a strain on the relationship. The effects tend to manifest themselves gradually though insecurities, irritability, and impatience. Even your partner's tiny quirks become the subject of heated discussions. Before you know it, you are subconsciously doubting and resenting each other. The worst thing is you don't even know where all these negative emotions are coming from, only that you're feeling them.

On the other hand, couples who have sex regularly are more easygoing and tolerant of each other's flaws. They are better able to sail smoothly through the daily trials they encounter in their relationship. Sex is a great stress-reliever and coming home after a hard day's work and getting some O's immediately pushes your buttons to love mode instead of battle mode. Furthermore, getting more O's can help you get better Zzz's and a great night's sleep leads to a fight-free morning. Couples find that once they get into fixing their bedroom issues, other issues in their marriage just sort of work themselves out.

> ➤ **Sex enables you to communicate with each other.**

When you're married or dating each other exclusively, sex is a language of love which you don't get to share with anyone else apart from your partner. There are some messages that are best expressed through touch and when you have sex with your spouse/lover, you tell him/her: *"I love you.", "I need you.",* and *"I want to be with you."*

Some couples think that as the sands of time screws up their libido, it becomes a message that it's time to start lying low. On the contrary, sex in marriage or in any long-term relationship doesn't have an expiration date. In fact, being together for so long gives you more excuses to get between the sheets more often. Why? Because your partner is that one person in this world who understands your body like no one else can. He/she has seen, touched, and loved every bit of you. Your long-time lover knows what makes you tick. He/she knows what makes you go wild and soft, what makes you feel alive, and what makes you feel loved. Each time you make love, you remind each other why you belong with each other and why no one else will do.

> ➤ **Sex helps you to build each other up.**

When you have sex, you tell your partner how much you value him/her. The mere act of initiating sex reassures your partner that you still find him/her attractive after all these years. When you show interest in each other, you boost each other's egos. When you offer yourselves to each other and marvel in its each other's bodies, it sends these messages: *"I'm happy to be yours."* and *"I'm proud that you're mine."*

> ➢ **Having sex more often keeps thoughts of infidelities away.**

If you start neglecting your partner, this negatively affects his/her self-esteem. This makes your spouse/lover wonder about the causes of your waning affection. Once a seed of doubt has been planted, there's no stopping its evil branches from growing. Her/his speculations may range from *"He's having an affair."* to *"She doesn't love me anymore."*

Furthermore, such undesirable thoughts can push either one of you to seek happiness, comfort, and pleasure somewhere else. This can lead you to explore dangerous what ifs and what-might-have-beens (example: *"What if I'd married my ex instead, maybe I would've been happier."* or *"I don't think it's my fault. I think I still got it. Maybe I should try it with someone else."*)

> ➢ **Having sex regularly helps you to grow old together *gracefully*.**

When one of you is suffering from a physical illness, the relationship also suffers. You'll spend too much time, thought, and energy into worrying about the medical bills and the future and when this happens, tenderness and affection takes a backseat. The fact is, when you're too preoccupied with your own pain, you don't have much care left in you to share with your partner. Moreover, couples with poor levels of health are prone to irritability and thus, making them vulnerable to domestic disputes.

A romp in the sheets is a fun and pleasurable way to burn calories. By turning sexy time into your cardio, you're helping each other stay physically fit. Regular sex reduces the risk of bone diseases (pun not intended), heart disease, and prostate cancer. Keep those hormones flowing to get the benefit of glowing skin and to tame those merciless menopausal symptoms. Sex is also a great immune system booster. Likewise, it enhances your capacity to deal with stress. Improve each other's health and prolong each other's lives so you can make more beautiful memories together.

Chapter 2

How to be Sexy in the Bedroom and How to Maintain a Great Sex Life

When you and your long-time lover have been at it for years, it has the following effects:

- less self-consciousness
- less mystery
- less spontaneity

> ➤ **Successful couples pay attention to pre-sex prepping.**

Your partner has seen it all so you shouldn't have to worry about shaving off your pubes, right? And since you love each other, it shouldn't matter if you skip the shower, right? Wrong! Being married for years and even being madly in love is no excuse for shortchanging your sexual soulmate. You need to perform pre-sex prepping as diligently as you did during the honeymoon phase of your relationship. Wear cologne like you used to. Invest in sexy lingerie like you used to. This will prevent your spouse from forgetting what attracted him/her to you in the first place. Furthermore, prepping your body for sex makes your partner feel special. It makes them feel that you still value what they think and that their desire is still worth earning.

The problem with some couples is that they find it awkward to talk to each other about sex and hygiene. To others, it's easier to just have sex less often than to risk embarrassing, provoking, or hurting their partner in a conversation about stubbles and body odors. So don't wait for your husband/wife to tell you that you need to take care of yourself because they probably won't. It's your job anyway and no one has to tell you to do these things. To put it bluntly: If you want more oral action, shave your nether regions.

That said, pre-sex prepping doesn't have to be a boring chore. In fact, you can even do it together. Start your foreplay in the shower by soaping each other's bodies.

> ➤ **Smart couples know that they have to look, think, feel, and be sexy.**

When you no longer find yourself attractive, this lowers your libido. Low self-esteem cripples your capacity to become open to new sexual adventures. A woman might be afraid of trying a new sex position because she's worried about how big her butt will look like. A man might feel threatened by prolonged foreplay because he might be unable to maintain his erection. In order to be sexy, you need to look, think, and feel the part. Preparing your body for sex shouldn't be done just prior to a lovemaking session. Instead, it should be something that you incorporate in your lifestyle. When you exercise, maintain a balanced diet, and rehydrate you are priming your body for lovemaking. A positive body image will make you more confident in bed. Provide yourself with positive affirmations (ex. "My body is beautiful.", "I am sexy within and without.")

Being physically fit will significantly improve your bedroom performance. Additionally, kegels exercises for women helps in toning the butt, the lower back, and the abdomen so she can effectively use these muscles to position herself during sex. Thus, allowing her to get more G-spot stimulation and more orgasms. Likewise, kegels exercises for men will help him in achieving ejaculatory control. Meanwhile, specific exercises like ball crunches can help improve his thrusting power.

> **Clever couples understand that familiarity breeds boredom.**

Sure, you've memorized every hair, every mole and explored every nook and cranny of each other's bodies but this is not an excuse to let the mystery jump out the window. Mystery equals to excitement and it's something that we all subconsciously crave. When this element disappears, that's when you start wondering and fantasizing about how it would feel like to have sex with other people. Not everyone will act on these fantasies but unfortunately, there are those who do.

To keep your spouse from straying, change things up in the bedroom. It doesn't have to be a drastic change. It can be as simple as a haircut or a new sex position that you haven't tried before. Readjust your carnal clock. That is, if you're used to making love in at night, rub up against your spouse early in the morning. Turn familiar objects and places into things and areas of mystery. Example: Make pantry staples even yummier by introducing food into foreplay. Surprise your spouse with an erotic buffet by placing fruits, whip cream, chocolate, and other edibles all over your body for him/her to feast on. Your partner will never see the kitchen in quite the same way.

> **A passive lover is no lover at all.**

So, are you a person or a blow-up doll? When you just lie there like you're bestowing your spouse a grand favor, you make your partner feel as though he/she is not worth your effort. This, in turn, kills their motivation, leading to mediocre performance. Furthermore, letting your partner do all the work implants in his/her brain that sex is nothing more than a routine activity. Remember that nothing can kill passion quicker than monotony. Motivate your partner by taking the lead from time to time. Sex should be a complete tactile, visual, and auditory experience. Even when your lover is on top, motivate him/her by sexy sounds and facial expressions. A woman can touch herself while her husband is making love to her. Likewise, a man can whisper words of affection (or talk dirty) while his wife is making love to him. Even when your partner is doing all the thrusting, do your part by stroking, kissing, and licking his/her erogenous spots. Moreover, eye contact deepens the intimacy of the act so even when you're all tied up, you can still participate by expressing your love (and lust) through your eyes.

> ### **Wise couples don't just do it. They talk about it.**

If there's anything that's more intimate than having sex, it's talking about sex. You become sexier to your partner if you can listen to his/her sexual suggestions with an open mind. Stay in tune with each other's erotic desires by openly discussing your fantasies and fetishes. Make a bucket list of the sex positions that you'd like to try, places that you'd like to have sex in, games and toys that you'd like to introduce in the boudoir, etc. Be sure to make this a fair give and take activity. When your partner feels that you're that one person in the world who can listen and make love to him/her without judgment and inhibitions, that's when you're at your sexiest.

Chapter 3

50 Best Sex Positions for Men and Women

Rear Entry Positions

Men love entering women from behind because this position feels very primal. Rear entry positions are also favorable for women who love a strong feeling of fullness during intercourse.

> ### ➢ Traditional Doggie Style

In this position, the woman gets down on her hands and knees with her legs somewhat apart. After this, the man positions himself on his knees and penetrates her from behind.

> ### ➢ Turtle Style

The woman kneels on the floor and then brings her body downwards. She does this so that her buttocks are lying on the back of her ankles. Next, she leans her body forward as far as it can go. The man then penetrates her from the rear.

> ### ➢ Frog Style

To do this, the woman should assume a squatting position. Then, she needs to lean forward. She should place her hands in front of her and make sure that they're flat on the floor. This will help her balance herself. Next, the man kneels behind her and enters her ala traditional doggie style.

> ### ➢ Basset Hound Style

The woman first positions herself on all fours. Next, she has to lower her body onto the floor, spreading her knees outward while pushing her buttocks up towards her partner. She then lowers herself to her elbows so that her chest is near the floor. Afterwards, the man penetrates her from behind.

➢ Corner Doggie Style

The woman assumes a standing position while placing one of her legs on either side of the bed corner. After this, she leans over toward the bed while supporting herself with her elbows. Next, the man enters her from the rear just as he would during the traditional doggie style.

➢ Rear Admiral Style

The couple starts off by standing while facing the same direction. Then, the man penetrates the woman from behind. After this, she bends over so that her abdomen is parallel to the ground. One of them should spread his/her legs open while the other keeps his/her own together. The couple can decide to take turns.

➢ Fire Hydrant Style

The first thing to do would be to have the woman position herself like she would in the traditional doggie style. Her partner should position himself behind her on his knees. He will then lift one of his legs, bring it forward, and place his foot on the ground to the woman's side. As he does this, he lifts her leg. This way, her thigh will be lying on top of his thigh.

➢ Bulldog Style

Compared to the classic doggie, the bulldog places the woman on a more submissive role. She gets down on her hands and her knees. Then the man and the woman have to bring their legs together. Afterwards, the man squats down a bit and then penetrates his partner from behind. His feet are situated outside of the woman's legs. Meanwhile, his hands are around her waist.

Deep Entry Positions that'll Make Husbands Go Crazy

Men love the feeling of going in deep into their partner. Apart from the exquisite physical pleasure that makes them want to ejaculate quickly, it provides them with a feeling of power and abandon.

➤ Anvil Style

In this position, the woman lies on her back. Meanwhile, she should keep her legs wide open. The man then lifts the woman's legs towards her chest. Afterwards, he moves over her, using his arms to support himself. Next, he asks her to rest her lower legs on either side of his head so they're touching his shoulders.

➤ Drill Style

The couple begins with the traditional missionary position, with the woman on her back and the man on top of her. Then, the woman spreads her legs. The man moves on top of the woman. As he does this, she draws up her legs and uses them to embrace her lover's waist.

➤ Deep Impact Style

Lying on her back, the woman points her legs skyward. Meanwhile, the man is to position himself on his knees facing her. Then, she rests her legs on each of her partner's shoulders. Next, he grabs her by the thighs and performs deep thrusts.

➤ Jockey Style

The couple begins by having the woman lie face down on the mattress. She's supposed to keep her legs together. Meanwhile, her lover straddles her, placing his knees on either side of her waist. This looks like he's riding a horse, hence the name. The jockey is perfect for either anal or vaginal penetration.

> ## Cello Player Style

This is done by having the woman lay on her back and then lift her legs in such a way that they're pointing upward. Meanwhile, the man should kneel upright while penetrating her. Next, the woman rests both her legs on *one* of her lover's shoulders. One of the man's arms is to be wrapped around the woman's lower leg. Meanwhile, his other arm should be wrapped around her thighs.

Dominant Male Positions

The following power positions are for men who like playing the role of the dom in the bedroom. These positions require the woman to be physically vulnerable and at his mercy, so to speak. He also gets total control of the pacing and the power of his thrusts. These are also perfect for women who like playing the role of the sub.

> ## Viennese Oyster Style

The woman lies down on her back and spreads her legs wide open. Grabbing her legs, she pulls them in towards herself until her knees are very close to the bed. Then, to make sure that her legs stay in place, she puts her arms at the back of her knees. The man then penetrates her.

> ## Down Stroke Style

The woman should be lying on the edge of the bed. She needs to raise her legs in the air so that they're pointing upward. Meanwhile, the man is to stand in front of the woman. He grabs the woman's legs and then pulls her body up towards his so he can enter her. Each time he thrusts downwards, he raises her body to meet his.

> ➢ **Bridge Style**

The woman should be on all fours. But here's the catch: Her back should be towards the ground and her body should be facing the ceiling. Facing his partner, the man kneels and positions himself between her legs. With his hands grabbing her thighs, he enters her while pulling her body close to his.

> ➢ **Suspended 69**

This is actually an exotic oral sex position that requires a great deal of power and flexibility. Be warned that this is a potentially dangerous position so it's not for everyone.

The man first lies down on his back. His feet, however, should be draped on the side of the bed, not so much as dangling, but with his feet played firmly on the floor. Next, his partner is to climb on top of him to position herself in a traditional 69. Keeping her legs together, she hugs her lover's head with them.

After a while, the man should try to sit up. Meanwhile, the woman is to make sure that her legs are still holding the back of her lover's neck. The next and the most crucial step would be to gauge whether it's still comfortable to perform oral sex on each other while maintaining this pose. Then, with the woman's arms embracing the man's waist, he gradually assumes a standing position.

Intimate Positions that Wives Love

Women particularly love sex positions that provide them not just with physical pleasure but also with a feeling of closeness with their partner.

> ## Spooning Style

The couple lies down on their sides while facing the same way. The man should be behind the woman. Then, he penetrates her from behind. The woman moves her top leg forward a bit to help the man enter her as he leans over. He then wraps her in his arms.

> ## Sporking Style

The couple starts by lying on their right side, with the man behind the woman. The woman then leans forward and takes her legs towards her upper torso.

> ## Side Entry Missionary Style

The woman needs to lie on her side while keeping her legs together and bending them a little. She may turn her body to face her partner who will have to be on top of her. He is to enter the woman from behind while he's positioned on his knees. So basically, it's like he's doing the missionary while his woman is in a side-lying position.

> ## Sofa Style

In this position, the man sits on the sofa with his feet flat on the floor. Facing him, the woman then squats on her partner and utilizes her legs to help her move up and down.

> ## Pearly Gates Style

Facing upward, the couple lies together. The man should bend his knees a little and make sure that his feet are planted on the mattress. The woman then lies on top of the man while still facing upward. So it's kind of like an upward version of spooning.

> ## Lotus Style

The man should be seated cross-legged, yoga style. Then, facing her partner, the woman lowers herself onto him. The man and the woman then wrap their arms around each other's bodies.

Positions to Give Women Multiple Orgasms

> ### Butterfly Style

While laying on her back, the woman's hips should be situated near the edge of the bed. The man stands at the foot of the bed and raises her hips, allowing her thighs to rest on his chest. The woman's lower legs should be resting on each of his shoulders.

> ### Criss Cross Style

Lying on her back, the woman raises her legs until they are pointing to the ceiling. Standing up straight, the man enters her. Making sure that the woman's legs are still straight, he crosses them at the ankles thus, creating a super tight fit.

> ### Fast Love Style

In this position, the man lies down with his knees slightly bent and his feet flat on the floor. The woman then straddles him while's she's on her feet. This is a nice quickie position for women who feel a sudden urge.

> ### Missionary Style

The woman lies on her back while keeping her legs open. Her partner positions himself on top of her in such a way that his legs are situated between hers. For support, the man may rest his elbows on either side of his partner.

Positions for Maximum G-spot Stimulation

➢ Bent Spoon Style

The man lies on his back and the woman lies on top of him, also on her back. This way, they're both looking up the ceiling. The man penetrates the woman. Meanwhile, she extends her arms outward. The man needs to keep his legs open. Then, the woman draws her knees up towards her upper body and allows her feet to rest on top of her lover's knees.

➢ Italian Hanger Style

The couples needs to first have sex in the classic missionary position. Then, somewhere during the middle, the man gets on his knees, bringing them close to his partner's body. As a result her legs will be spread wider apart. Then, he places his hands beneath her buttocks and raises her hips. He then proceeds with his thrusts.

Positions for Maximum Clitoral Stimulation

➢ Coital Alignment Technique

The woman lies on her back with her partner on top of her. How is this different from the missionary? He has to move his body forward over the woman's as opposed to thrusting in and out of her. This changes the angle of penetration so that his penis is able to stimulate her lower vaginal wall. This way, his pubic bone is in direct contact with her clitoris.

➢ Thigh Tide Style

Lying on his back, the man tries to keep his legs straight while spreading them to some degree. Then, he lifts one knee in such a way that his foot is planted firmly on the mattress. The woman straddles his raised knee and lowers herself onto her lover's penis with her back against him. Then, she performs up and down movements, which will allow her to rub her clitoris against her partner's thighs.

> ## Sandwich Style

The man penetrates the woman ala missionary style while's she's lying on her back with her legs spread open and pulled back towards her chest. He then places one hand under each of her knees to adjust the angle of penetration.

Woman-on-Top Positions for Fierce Females

Women enjoy these positions because it provides them with a sense of empowerment and allows them to control the pace of lovemaking thus, enabling them to achieve orgasms. Men also love woman-on-top positions because it enables them to relax and just open themselves up for pleasure. Additionally, it provides them with a sensational view of their partner's body.

> ## Cowgirl Style

The man lies down on his back while the woman assumes a kneeling position as she straddles him. Her legs are supposed to be situated on either side of her lover's waist. She then proceeds to bouncing up and down or grinding on top of him. By moving her body backward or forward, she is able to regulate the angle of penetration.

> ## Reverse Cowgirl Style

This is pretty much the same as the cowgirl style. The main difference is that the woman has her back to her partner as she straddles him and bounces or grinds on top of him.

➢ Asian Cowgirl Style

This is another variation of the cowgirl sex position. The major difference is that the woman squats with her feet on either side of her lover's body instead of being on her knees. Her feet will therefore be carrying her weight. Her hands may rest on her partner's chest or on either side of him.

➢ Bucking Bronco Style

While the man lies on his back, the woman faces him and then gets on top of him. She then guides his penis inside her. After he has penetrated her, she leans backwards while placing her arms behind her. After this, she places her feet on either side of her partner's head.

➢ Rodeo Style

This sex position is a variation of the reverse cowgirl. Facing towards her partner's feet, the woman straddles him while on her knees. The man's job here is to thrust really hard and fast, almost as if he's attempting to buck his partner off him. Meanwhile, she holds on tight and rides the rodeo!

➢ Amazon Style

In this dominant woman-on-top position, the woman asks her partner to lie on his back and tells him to draw his legs up and bend his knees. As he pulls his legs towards his upper torso, she squats down on him and carefully pulls his penis backwards to guide him inside her.

➢ Crab Style

While lying on his back, the man should keep his legs together. The woman then straddles him, placing her legs on either side of his body. After this, she leans backward with her hands and arms extended behind her. She makes love to him by moving her body up and down while using her arms for support. She may also choose to perform rotating maneuvers with her hips.

> ## ➢ Missionary Style with Woman on Top

This is different from the traditional missionary style because the woman will be taking the top position. The woman should first ask her partner to lie down with his legs straight. Then, she straddles him while on her knees. Next, she leans her body forward and rests her elbows on the bed.

Man-on-Top Positions for Women who Love Dominant Men

Women love having sex with men who are confident and know what they're doing in bed. By taking control, he is allowing her to just relax and focus on receiving pleasure.

> ## ➢ Cowboy Style

While on her back, the woman makes sure that she keeps her legs together as her partner straddles her. The man's legs are situated on either side of her body. Meanwhile his bum is resting right on top of his partner's legs.

> ## ➢ Deckchair Style

The couples start off in the missionary position. Then, the man gets into his knees while inserting his arms under the each of the woman's knees. His hands are placed on the bed for support. Meanwhile, the woman remains positioned on her back while raising her legs into the air. By assuming this position, they get to stimulate areas that don't get much attention when having sex in the traditional missionary position.

> ### Launch Pad Style

The woman lies on her back. Meanwhile, the man is on his knees facing her. He enters her and as he does this, she raises her legs skyward, drawing her knees towards her upper body. Then, she allows her feet to rest on her partner's chest.

> ### Victory Style

The man is on top while the woman lies on her back and spreads her legs open, holding it up in a V shape. The man then performs thrusting movements while on his knees.

> ### Exposed Eagle Style

It's best to begin this position with the classic cowgirl. Once there, the woman leans backward until her back is on top of her lover's knees and his thighs. Then, the man lifts the upper part of his body so that he's seated upright.

Quickie Positions

Nothing turns on a man or a woman more than knowing that his/her sex soulmate wants to have sex with him/her anytime, anywhere. As such, you must have an arsenal of quickie sex positions up your sleeve.

> ### Bodyguard Style

Couples start off by standing upright and facing the same way. The man should be positioned behind the woman. Then, with the back part of her body pressed against his front, he penetrates her from behind.

> ### Bendover Style

The couple first performs the bodyguard sex position. After he's inside her, she leans her body forward with her arms extended. She lowers her body until her hands are resting on the ground. Then, the man starts thrusting in and out of her.

> ### Burning Man Style

This sex position is best done on a countertop. The woman bends over so that her tummy is resting over the countertop. Meanwhile, her feet should be planted firmly on the floor. This will help keep her in place because this position is designed for hard and fast thrusting, hence the name. Her partner then proceeds to entering her from the rear. Couples can use this whether they want to make love vaginally or anally.

> ### Dancer Style

The couple stands facing each other. Then, the woman raises one of her legs and envelops her man's body with it. Next, the man penetrates her and begins thrusting. To make sure that his partner stays in place, the man may wrap his arms around her while supporting her raised leg with his hand.

> ### Pump Style

If you want to have sex by a wall, perform this position by having the woman assume a sitting position in the air. The woman's legs should be bent a little. The man stands beside her and penetrates her from the rear. He then proceeds to thrusting in and out while grabbing onto her waist. To keep herself steady, she may extend her arms and press them against the wall.

Conclusion

Thank you again for downloading this book!

I hope this book was able to help you to understand and appreciate the value of sex in keeping relationships alive.

The next step is to apply these bedroom tips and to try out these sex positions to help lovemaking become the exciting, fulfilling, and nurturing experience that it's supposed to be. May this be the beginning of a fun and intimate adventure between you and your significant other.

Finally, if you enjoyed this book, then I'd like to ask you for a favor, would you be kind enough to leave a review for this book on Amazon? It'd be greatly appreciated!

Thank you and good luck!

Made in the USA
San Bernardino, CA
24 May 2018